WHY PARENTS SECRETLY HATE CHILDREN'S BIRTHDAY PARTIES

A PRACTICAL GUIDE OF HOW TO PLAN, HOST, SURVIVE, AND ENJOY PLANNING BIRTHDAY PARTIES FOR KIDS.

ASHIA WATSON

Party Sticklers
Events & Design

WHY PARENTS SECRETLY HATE CHILDREN'S BIRTHDAY PARTIES. Copyright © 2017 by Ashia Watson

Party Sticklers, LLC
44050 Ashburn Shopping Plaza
Suite 195-111
Ashburn, VA 20147
www.partysticklers.com

Manufactured in the United States of America. All rights reserved. No part of this book may be reproduced, distributed, or transmitted in any form or by any means including photocopying, recording, or electronic or mechanical methods, without the prior written permission of the author. The only exception is in the case of brief quotations embodied in critical reviews and certain noncommercial uses permitted by copyright law.

Any Internet addresses (websites, blogs, products, companies, etc.) printed in this book are offered as a resource and are not intended in any way to be or to imply an endorsement. This publication contains opinions and ideas of the author. The strategies outlined in this book may not be suitable for every individual and are not guaranteed or warranted to produce any particular results. The author expressly disclaims any liability, loss, or risk, personal or otherwise which is incurred as a consequence, direct or indirect of the use or application of the contents of the book.

Contact the Author: letstalk@partysticklers.com

Design Cover: Oliviaprodesign/Depositphotos

Author Photos: Studio Plus

Other Photos: Page 1: dreamstime.com/Juan Moyano, Page 10: dreamstime.com/Ruth Black

Editor: Cathy Oasheim, Oasheim Editing Services, LLC

ISBN-13: 978-0-9997606-0-4
ISBN-13: 978-0-9997606-1-1
LCCN: 2018940065

Printed in the United States of America

CONTENTS

INTRODUCTION 9

CHAPTER 1: Party Mom Personality Traits 11
What Type of Party Mom Are You? 11
The Rookie Mom 13
Party Hater Mom 13
Party Blues Mom 14
Party Pooper Mom 14
Last-Minute Mom 15
Lifesaver Mom 16
Drive-By Mom 16
Diva Mom 17
Supermom 17
The Joneses Mom 18
It's Not About you Mom 19

CHAPTER 2: Let's Get This Party Started 21
So You Want to Plan a Party 21
Fear of Party Hosting 21
Weddings in Disguise 22
Is Bigger Better? 22
Don't Keep Score 23
Throwback Birthday Parties 23
First Birthday Party Debate 23
Failing to Plan Is Planning to Fail 24
Morning Parties 25
Don't Break the Piggy Bank 25

Money Talks 26
Is it Time to Consider a Party Planner? 27
Why Hire a Party Planner? 27
Parties Are Not FREE 29
Stay in Your Lane 29
Bang for your Buck 30
Event Timeline 31

CHAPTER 3: The Perfect Venue 33
Location, Location, Location 33
Home Parties versus Venues 33
Unique Venues 34
Cookie Cutter Venues 34
Read the Fine Print 35

CHAPTER 4: You're Invited 37
Who's Coming? 37
The More the Merrier? Wrong 37
Child's Age + 1 38
The School Dilemma 38
Custom Invitations 39
Electronic Invitations 39
The Dreaded RSVP 40
Accepts with Pleasure 40
Regrets Only 40
Non-Transferable Guests 41
Chasing Down Guests 41
Final Headcount 42

CHAPTER 5: Let Them Eat 43

Playing Master Chef 43

Airplane Food 43

Fancy Foods 43

Stain-Free Parties 44

Food Allergies 44

Pre-Made Cakes 45

Fondant Anyone? 45

CHAPTER 6: Are Good Manners Extinct? 47

RSVP Already 47

Siblings 47

Drop-Off or Not? 49

No-Shows 50

Party of One 52

Party Crashers 52

Dealing with Late Guests 53

Sick Kids 55

Early Birds 55

Latecomers 55

Parents Staying 56

Small Talk 56

Hungry Parents 57

Pick Up your Kids 57

CHAPTER 7: The Devil Is In The Details 59

Don't Believe the Hype 59

Get Unplugged 59

To DIY or Not to DIY? 60

Shop with Purpose 60

CHAPTER 8: The Goody Bag Debate 63
Where's My Goody Bag? 63
Trash the Goody Bag 64
Alternative Party Favors 64

CHAPTER 9: Birthday Gifts 67
Pass the Present-Buying Baton 67
How Much to Spend 67
No Gifts Please 68
Charitable Gifts 68
Gift Registry Debate 69
Gift Card Debate 69
Gift Opening Debate 70

CHAPTER 10: It's Party Time–Let's Do This 73
Bulletproof Parties (Keep Dreaming) 73
Delegate, Delegate, Delegate 73
The Early Bird Gets the Worm 73
Plan B (Backup Contingency Plan) 74

CHAPTER 11: The After Party 75
The Dreaded Cleanup 75
Need Help? So, Ask for Help 75
Cleanup after Yourself 76
Hire a Cleaning Service 76
To Send or Not to Send 77

CHAPTER 12 The Good, Bad, and Ugly 79
Love It or Hate It 79

THANK YOU 81
PRAISE FOR WHY PARENTS SECRETLY HATE CHILDREN'S BIRTHDAY PARTIES 83
ACKNOWLEDGMENTS 87
ABOUT THE AUTHOR 89

INTRODUCTION

Despite what you think, no exact science or playbook exists for event planning. Before I dive into this book, I will tell you my story as a party planner. Folks, I have seen and heard it all–parents trying to please others, competition, stress, anxiety, and frustrations of parents trying to plan a party. I'm writing this book to share helpful information about the children's birthday party world. I will chime in on unpopular and debatable topics we love to hate. In this book, you will get the real deal with no added sugar coating, and a no-nonsense approach to party planning.

Why Parents Secretly Hate Children's Birthday Parties will be playful, fun, and not a boring read (I hope). Just an early disclaimer, I am old school with party etiquette, but I embrace new school and modern etiquette models when it makes balancing my life easier. I don't apologize and I am guilty as charged. Be warned, the etiquette topics may be hot, controversial, and debatable. As parents, we can agree to disagree.

Everyone loves children's birthday parties, right? Wrong. So, what's the big deal? It isn't every day that your child gets to celebrate their birthday. Toddlers, tweens, teens, adults, grandparents, and people all over the world celebrate birthdays. So, what's the love-hate relationship parents have with children's birthday parties? The truth is many parents do not have the time, energy, patience, finances, or the creativity to plan and execute a lavish or simply elegant children's party. For many parents, the idea of children's parties equal stress, extra expenses, and headaches instead of fun and memories.

Don't feel ashamed. You can love your children and hate the logistics of party planning. Gone are the days of parents inviting children over to their home for a birthday party, with no formal activities and games, and the children just run around and have fun. Nowadays, children's parties range from $500 to over $5000, depending on the number of guests, and the complexity of the event. I know this might give you a headache or make you want to pull out your stress ball just thinking of everything involved. Pulling off an amazing children's party, with sleepless nights and no professional help, can push any parent over the edge.

Can party planning be stressful and intense? Sure, but it shouldn't be so stressful that it causes you to have a panic attack. There's no one-size-fits-all answer to the stressful and difficult situations when planning a party. Each party is different and so are the challenges that come with it.

The good news is that *Why Parents Secretly Hate Children's Birthday Parties* will give you useful tips to make you well equipped to handle the roadblocks and hurdles of party planning. It provides the ins and outs of planning a successful party and tips on how you can enjoy the process. If you love hosting parties, this book gives you more insight into the eyes of parents. If you hate attending children's birthday parties, I hope you will have a change of heart after reading this book. With the right state of mind and realistic goals, the planning process can be fun and stress-free. This book provides honest guidance and tips on how to handle certain stressful situations in the planning process. Are you ready to get this party started? Cheers to planning a fabulous party.

CHAPTER 1
Party Mom Personality Traits

What Type of Party Mom Are You?

Party planning brings out different emotions in people. Are you a rock star party planner or do you prefer to hide under a rock? Do you thrive with organized chaos or become stressed and anxious? These different personality traits are normal feelings of how people cope with the excitement or frustrations of planning a children's birthday party.

In this chapter, you will find a variety of different party mom personality traits. I've listed a few of my favorites. Can you identify what type of party mom you are? You may fit into one category, multiple categories, or none. Before you choose which personality trait best suits you, answer the questions below. Try to dig deep and figure out why you love or hate parties. Experiences often shape our perceptions. I encourage you to answer the questions to understand and learn how you handle stress. Acceptance is the first step to recovery from our current perceptions. If you identify with any of these traits, you are not alone. Come on and try it. What do you have to lose?

1) What is one word that describes how you feel about children's birthday parties?

2) Have you ever been hurt, embarrassed, sad, left out, or isolated at a party?

3) What do you enjoy the most about birthday parties?

4) Do you prefer intimate or large birthday parties?

5) Do you love or hate birthday parties as an adult?

6) What do you hate about birthday parties?

7) What stresses you out the most about parties?

8) Do you hate mingling and the small talk at birthday parties?

9) What is your biggest fear of planning an event?

10) Do you compete with your family, friends, or classroom moms when planning parties?

11) Are you influenced or care what other parents think?

12) Do you limit the number of parties your child may attend?

The Rookie Mom

If you're a mother, you can relate to the Rookie Mom. We've been and seen that mom. This is the mom fresh out the hospital and waiting for the how-to parent manual for babies. She later realizes no book exists, except for good old fashion trial and error. The Rookie Mom is new to the children's party planning world. Sure, these moms may have attended or even assisted their friend, niece, or nephew's birthday party, but they never planned one on their own. Planning a birthday party for your own child is on another level. If you love sports, it resembles a player being in the game and the other being on the bench. If you're on the bench, you're only a seat warmer and spectator watching the game, but you can't experience the butterflies, adrenaline rush, fear, and pressure of being in the game. With research, practice, and help from family and friends, new moms and Rookie Moms will soon be playmakers instead of benchwarmers.

☐ Yes, that's me
☐ No, I can't relate

Party Hater Mom

Are you a mom that doesn't get energized by being around large groups and unfamiliar faces? Do you prefer to be by yourself or with close friends? Do you hate attending and planning children's birthday parties? Party Hater Moms are gasping for air at the thought of having to plan or attend a birthday party. These moms don't like being around large crowds, would rather be alone, and don't have the desire to engage in small talk and meet new parents. For some moms, they feel like they're walking on eggshells and interviewing to be in a mom's secret society. If you happen to spark a conversation, you might get a quick one-phrase sentence. The Party Hater Mom is checking her phone non-stop to only be disappointed that only an hour has passed and she still has one hour to go.

Birthday parties have become a rite of passage for children. For parents, it's a non-stop event that you may have to endure one or two times a month. For parents, the novelty and thought of hosting a birthday party have worn off and many moms have anxiety and fatigue. For some moms, it's hard work. Ladies, I get it, birthday parties are stressful and overwhelming.

What mom really wants to keep track of each child's food allergies, who is picking up little Johnny, and having to deal with the different personalities of the kids *and* parents? It can also be awkward when you don't know the parents or don't care to know the parents. The Party Hater Mom can fall into several personality traits but at the end of the day, this mom wants nothing to do with a children's birthday party. You are not alone Party Hater Mom. You are the perfect candidate to hire a professional party planner so you can just show up and not even lift your finger.

☐ Yes, that's me
☐ No, I can't relate

Party Blues Mom

Does entertaining make you stressed and give you the blues? Do you suffer from birthday party burnout? If so, it's time to analyze the steps of what you're doing and how you can improve. You've made your party list and checked it twice. Your list continues to get longer but you don't have enough time or energy to complete everything before the big day. You dread the days of wasting gas, and the thought of dragging your kids in and out of different stores. The hassle of trying to hunt down party decorations is giving you second thoughts. This book provides you the encouragement, tools, and tips you need to plan a successful children's party without losing your mind.

☐ Yes, that's me
☐ No, I can't relate

Party Pooper Mom

Are you a party pooper with children's birthday parties? Do you limit how many birthday parties your child can attend? Do you only allow your child to attend children's birthday parties of parents in your circle? If you answered yes to any of these questions, welcome to the club. You will find the Party Pooper Mom sitting on the sideline, ready and waiting to go home. If this personality trait speaks to you,

you are not alone. A lot of moms fall into this category for different reasons. The good news is that you're in for a ride with this book. As a party planner, I understand the emotional roller coaster parents experience when planning their child's party. My goal is to make your life much easier with valuable resources, helpful tips, and strategies.

☐ Yes, that's me
☐ No, I can't relate

Last-Minute Mom

Are you the mom who is always late starting the party or attending the party? Are you addicted to the adrenaline rush or thrill of being late? Do you try to cram in last-minute errands to maximize every second and minute of the day? Are you an attention seeker or want to be the center of attention everywhere you go? The popular phrase by Lik Hock Yap Ivan, "If you're early, you're on time. If you're on time, you're late" doesn't apply to these moms. When I say late, I don't mean 15-30 minutes late, but hours late. Last-minute moms are on cruise control and island time. You've seen the type; the moms where the party doesn't start until they arrive. The Last-Minute Mom always arrives late to a children's birthday party. You will find the Last-Minute Mom running into the store 5 minutes before the party to get a gift. Many moms have endless excuses for why they're late or never show up. It's not cool to be fashionably late, and it's not in style. Don't arrive at parties late and make your guests wait on your behalf. It's an unpopular habit that many people view as rude and impolite. Make the most of your time and respect other people's time; plan to be early. Guests should be culturally sensitive to the applicable etiquette of the hosts of the party.

Create a strategy for getting things done on time. Buy a watch, set your internal clock, set your phone alarm, and plan ahead. Stay away from making any detours or last-minute errands when you know you need to leave the house. Make the most of your time. Running late happens to everyone, but don't make it routine.

☐ Yes, that's me
☐ No, I can't relate

Lifesaver Mom

Are you a Lifesaver Mom? This mom is a lifesaver to busy parents or single mothers juggling and taking multiple kids to different places when they can't be in two places at the same time. The Lifesaver Mom is the official taxi driver for the neighborhood kids except she doesn't get paid for it. She is the head honcho for dropping off the kids and picking them up. The Lifesaver Mom is loved and respected by her community but often feels neglected. This mom can get stressed and overwhelmed with the responsibility of shuffling her children and other children around. Be sure to share the taxi driver responsibilities with other parents. The goal in carpooling is that both parties get a break without the kids.

☐ Yes, that's me
☐ No, I can't relate

Drive-By Mom

Are you a Drive-By Mom at parties? The Drive-By Mom drops off her child, kicks them out the car while waving or giving them the *peace out* or *deuces* sign, and jetting out of sight while screaming, "I'm Out!". The Drive By Mom values her free time so you most likely won't catch her lingering around and hanging out at the party with the kids, or offer to help out. As your children get older, most moms turn into the Drive By Mom. The Drive By Mom loves children's birthday parties because it means her children are not with her. We love our children but sometimes we want and need a break to keep our sanity in check. Birthday parties allow parents to have a break without the kids attached to their hip. There's something so tranquil and peaceful when you can sit in the house in silence when the kids are not home. Try it sometime and you will see what I mean.

Many Drive By Moms are in a rush to get errands done, head to the grocery store, take a nap, get a manicure or pedicure, and go on a quick date with her hubby or boyfriend. In the eyes of a Drive By Mom, a birthday party equals free babysitting and no kids for two to three hours. It's the same feeling you get when your child goes outside to play for hours. This only applies when your children are at the appropriate age for drop off. Please don't drop off your child if they are a toddler or younger in age (five and under). That's pushing the limitations of the unspoken free babysitting rules. One more thing, please don't abuse your privileges by being early to drop your child off, and late picking them up. These are grounds for being banned from the guest list for future parties.

☐ Yes, that's me
☐ No, I can't relate

Diva Mom

Are you a Diva Mom? The Diva Mom is slaying it with her designer outfit, handbag, and killer stiletto heels that make you want to ditch wearing your flats if your feet wouldn't hurt so much. Who cares if stilettos are not good for your feet, they're hot! You will never catch the diva mom sporting yoga pants, messy hair in a bun, and no makeup. The Diva Mom is always on top of her fashion game and looks so fresh and clean. However, many diva moms get the side eye from other moms if they are dressed as if they're headed to the club instead of a children's birthday party. That's not a good look.

☐ Yes, that's me
☐ No, I can't relate

Supermom

Are you a Supermom? The mom that is all hands-on-deck and a professional multi-tasker. A Supermom can do no wrong in the eyes of parents. She's the mom we all love to hate. The real truth is that Supermoms are fatigued, exhausted, and overwhelmed but you would never know. She takes on more than she can bear being a wife, mother, friend, teacher, chef, taxi driver, tax accountant, and housekeeper. The Supermom juggles many tasks on her own because in her mind she thinks she can do it all. She has the mindset of if she doesn't do it, it won't be done right. Supermoms think they don't need a party planner. Think again; novice, intermediate, and professional experts can all benefit from a party planner. Embrace the fact that no one can do it on their own. You're not running a marathon to be the best mom ever and you definitely won't be a contender if you end up in the hospital because of a panic attack or nervous breakdown. How is that going to be beneficial to your family? It's okay to say no or take off your cape and delegate tasks to your family, friends, and children. Your children won't remember you forgot to make the brownies shaped like race cars, but they will remember mommy was stressed, frantic, and angry at the party. The death of a party happens when parents try to do everything…hosting and facilitating, cooking, cleaning, baking, and playing DJ. Sometimes you need to step back, call it quits, and take off your cape when your cool card gets revoked because you've turned into the frantic mom instead of the fun mom. Hiring a party planner will save your sanity. You can still be a Supermom but not at the expense of your health.

☐ Yes, that's me
☐ No, I can't relate

The Joneses Mom

Have you ever attended a children's birthday party and was envious, guilty, or compared your party to another party your child attended? Do you feel inferior when you're around a specific mom? Do you need approval from other moms? You've heard the popular phrase, "Keeping up with the Joneses"? Each year, The Joneses Mom throws bigger and more elaborate parties to appease their child, friends, and family. With the popularity of lavish and unique children's birthday parties, parents are not only trying to keep up and compete with the Joneses, but most times they *are the Joneses*, trying to compete with themselves. Every year more parents confess they are trying to impress their family, friends, and business partners by topping last year's epic party. Topping last year's party is sometimes unrealistic and hard to carry out. When will the jealousy and competition end? Pump your brakes and listen to what your child wants. Don't give into the temptations of competing with your family and friends. Remember, you don't need approval from other moms. You only need approval from the person who matters the most; your child.

☐ Yes, that's me
☐ No, I can't relate

It's Not About you Mom

Are you the mom that forces your favorite party theme on your child? Do you not care what your child wants because you're paying for the party? Do you care more about the adults than the children attending the party? Nowadays, moms will find any reason to celebrate an event in the name of the children. Sometimes hosting a children's party is an excuse for adults to get together. The parties are adult parties disguised as children's parties. I love big family bashes but a lot of parents don't take the time to include their child in the party planning process. Involving your child is important for a successful party. Not only will the birthday boy or girl be more excited, the enjoyment, involvement, and anticipation for the party will be greater. The last thing you want is for children to be bored at a children's birthday party when it's primarily adults in attendance. A party should be fun for everyone. Hire a party planner to ensure your children's party is entertaining for both the kids and adults.

☐ Yes, that's me
☐ No, I can't relate

PARTY PLANNING SURVIVAL TIPS

☐ The secret for stress-free parties is planning ahead.

☐ Invent your own party theme.

☐ Build your party around the theme.

☐ Set boundaries and let go of competition and social obligations.

CHAPTER 2
Let's Get This Party Started

So You Want to Plan a Party

It's time to plan your next party. Do you cringe at throwing a party because you don't have one artistic bone in your body, or you're not a natural-born party planner? The unknown tasks overwhelm you, and you don't even know where to start. The emotions and stress you are feeling at this moment are natural and common. These feelings may come and go with proper planning. In fact, most people aren't natural party planners. The good news is that party planning is a skill you can learn through training, repetition, and practice.

Fear of Party Hosting

For many parents, hosting a party at their home is more stressful than a job interview. They are self-conscious hosting parties in their home and are fearful of being scrutinized, criticized, and judged by their family and friends. People come up with different excuses for why they can't host a party at their home: "Our home is not big enough to entertain", "The furniture is old and outdated", and "Our home is too dirty to have company."

Let's be real, the only time many of our homes get a deep cleaning is when we're hosting a party at our home. For many parents, all the hard work and housekeeping you did for your home to regress back to an unclean state after the party, is not fun. Stop caring what other people think and say because not everyone will love your home. When hosting parties, don't focus on your materialistic things. Who cares how big your house is or that you own high-end furniture. Whether you live in a studio apartment or a mini-mansion, anyone can host a party in their home. Reconnecting and engaging with your family and friends is the goal.

Weddings in Disguise

Similar to superheroes, many children's birthday parties are disguised as mini weddings in the making. Beyond the dress, tuxedo, and rings, children's parties resemble weddings. I'm joking, but there lies the truth. Just think about it for a minute. A wedding and children's party have more in common than not. You need a firm budget, date, time, venue, guests, save the dates, invitations, RSVPs, food and beverages, dessert and cake, activities, music, entertainment, party favors, setup and decorating, breakdown, cleanup, thank you cards, and the list goes on and on.

Nowadays, every birthday is a milestone event that is celebrated. Parents are living in the moment and going all out. Children's parties have uniformed waitstaff, finger foods served on silver platters, specialty three-tiered cake, and live entertainment. Some children's birthday parties cost more than weddings. You can stay in denial but folks, it is the new normal. More parents are jumping on the bandwagon to host these extravagant parties. It can be a vicious cycle of competition. Some parents love the glitz and glam of children's birthday parties while other parents feel uncomfortable and inadequate.

Is Bigger Better?

Is bigger better? No, no, and no. I hate to break it to you, but you're not winning the 'Parent-of-the-Year' award for inviting the entire fifth-grade class. For party planning, the bigger the event, the more stress and money you will spend. Birthday parties are about the memories you create and cherish with your family and friends. Planning a children's party has its challenges, but the details can make or break your party. Celebrating your child's birthday and having fun should be your highest priority. For children's parties, people remember the personalization, decorations, and fun factor. Your party doesn't have to be large to be memorable. Always plan your party with the one thought in mind, "FUN". Hire a children's party planner to handle the details and entertainment.

Don't Keep Score

Many parents give into the party pressure of competing with their child's classmates, family, and friends. The drama that unfolds with these parties can get easily out of control. Parents are competing for the affections of their child and their classmate friends. They are also trying to go bigger and better with a competing mom. Some moms even book parties on the same day of a competitor mom. Who are you trying to impress? Why do you care what other parents say or think? If a parent imitates and copies your party why are you mad? Instead, be flattered that the parent loved your party so much that they want to mimic what you did. Children's birthday parties are for celebrating the child, not for competition. Don't keep score or try to one-up other parents. End of story.

Throwback Birthday Parties

What happened to the good old days where you invited two to four of your best friends, ordered a pizza, ate junk food, watched movies, played board games and truth or dare, sang songs and danced, or stayed up late? Do you mourn for these simplistic parties? The secret ingredient for these parties is the fun factor and extra sugar.

First Birthday Party Debate

Are you debating whether to host a first birthday party for your child? There are many debatable opinions and perspectives on this topic. Should you host an intimate family event or a big shindig? Ask yourself, who wants to attend a first birthday party? You got it, family, family, family, and close friends. Not to mention, your child has no friends and can't take part in any activities without help from an adult. Will your child remember the party? No, your one-year-old will not remember you handmade the perfect birthday cake from scratch. When your children get older they will appreciate and relive the party through your stories, pictures, and videos later. Children love seeing themselves in print and on video. All life is worth celebrating so my vote is yes for throwing a first birthday party. What do you think?

Failing to Plan Is Planning to Fail

The old quote from Benjamin Franklin, "Failing to plan is planning to fail" speaks volumes when planning an event. Whether you're planning for a few or hundreds of guests, you have to plan, prep, and prepare. No matter the size, the end goal is the same. Procrastination will kill the success of any party. Start slowly with one project at a time. Check off each completed task on your checklist. Drop the excuses for why you are not preparing and planning. You must prepare for unexpected expenses and surprises. During the preliminary stages of planning, create a realistic budget, party checklist, food menu, grocery store shopping list, event timeline, and day of event checklist to track your progress. Your shopping list should include the party décor supplies and props needed to pull off the party theme. The day of the party you should follow your event timeline. The time slots are not written in stone. If you take thirty minutes for the games, instead of the twenty minutes you allocated, you can always make up the time when you serve the food or while cutting the cake.

Are you a last minute planner? Are you overwhelmed when you wait until the last-minute to put your party together? It's amazing how a birthday party can creep up on you. Before you know it, invitations must be sent and it becomes a frantic frenzy chasing people who did not RSVP and getting organized at the last minute. With a little forward planning, the whole process will become smoother and less stressful. Take the time to sit down and plan out the party. You can also use this opportunity to brainstorm ideas for decorations, games, food, cake, dress up costumes, entertainment, and music.

Stay away from planning last-minute parties. Plan in advance to avoid extra fees and the stress which comes with leaving things until the last minute. Keep in mind, last-minute parties often incur more fees to make sure the party décor and supplies will arrive on time. Plan your party six to eight weeks in advance. Popular children's party planners book one to three months in advance and six months for formal parties.

Morning Parties

For children's parties, timing is everything. The time you choose is important if you want your guests to attend. Many parents dislike mid-day parties because it takes up most of their day where they could knock out other errands and activities. Likewise, a morning party is not fun for parents that prefer to sleep. Sometimes the weekends are the only time parents get extra sleep. No parent wants to wake up early on their day off to bring their child to a birthday party. Be warned, you may have more latecomers or no-shows if you host an early morning party. The best time for a morning party is 11:00 am. Morning parties do not need full meals but you can offer light breakfast treats, snacks, or brunch. Who doesn't love donuts? That's right, pump the kids full of sugar and give them back to their parents.

Don't Break the Piggy Bank

Please don't spend your child's college money to fund a birthday party. If you don't have the money, don't spend the money. Be realistic and scale down if necessary. Doing the party yourself may seem like a great idea, but in the end could cost you more money and stress. Avoid falling for those puppy dog eyes or the blank stare your child will give you to get their way. Stay strong and do not give into your child's temper tantrums and comparisons with other friends. Resist giving in and spending over your budget. The amount of fun children have at a party does not necessarily relate to how much money you spend. Ask yourself how much you can afford. Anticipate the expenses which may arise while planning for the party so there are no surprises. Be sure your budget is realistic and you can afford all the expenses. If not, don't ask your vendors to lower their prices. You will need to scale down, reduce your cost, cut items, or find another affordable vendor. If you can't afford it, don't spend it. Asking vendors to lower their prices is devaluing their services and worth. Are you willing to take a reduction in your salary?

Ask yourself, what is most important to you. Don't expect to have everything on your wish list if you're on a budget. Choose what you want, need, and can afford for your party. Unless you have an unlimited budget, the cost of planning and executing an event can be very expensive, and the price can creep up on you if you're not careful to stick to your budget.

Children's birthday parties don't have to be over the top like "My Super Sweet 16" from MTV. Parents spending $10,000-$50,000 on a children's birthday party is far from reality for most families. Don't take out a second mortgage to finance your child's party. Unfortunately, children often don't understand money and how much the things they want cost. Help your children understand their party will still be fun, but on a smaller scale. Be open and honest with your children about your finances and how it affects the things they want for the party. Don't be vague and be firm with your children to stay within your budget. Find ways to stretch your money so your child doesn't feel like they're missing out.

Money Talks

How do you want to spend the major share of your budget? Do you want to spend it on event planning, decorating, food, entertainment, music, catering, or cake? My vote is for decorating, decorating, decorating. Come on, what did you expect me to say? I cast my vote for decorating because your guests will remember the decorations. Most guests will take pictures of the party décor and these images will stay in their memory for years to come. Whenever your guests look back at the pictures from your event, guess what they will see? You're correct, decorations, decorations, decorations. Everything else is an after-thought and blur for your guests. Many guests won't remember the small details of the decorations, other guests will remember every little detail, down to whether your LED candles looked realistic and flickered, or not.

In order to keep spending in control, set your budget before you plan. Is it possible a professional party planner can save you money? Yes, it is. They have an abundance of party décor and props in their inventory and at their finger tips. Get the high-end look for less by hiring a party planner or event stylist. You will most likely not be able to recreate the look and find the exact décor they have in their inventory. Not to mention, you have limited time to find all the décor when your child's birthday party is in less than a month.

Is it Time to Consider a Party Planner?

Does party planning make you stressed, frustrated, anxious, restless, not sleeping well at night, and snapping at others? Is hiring a party planner worth your sanity? Yes, yes, and yes. Party planners can eliminate the stress by doing the leg work and running around for you. You'll have a professional event planner on your team before the party begins, after the party ends, and everything in between. You can bounce off ideas and get realistic feedback. Seriously, who wouldn't want a personal party shopper to hand pick the decorations, supplies, setup, decorate, and cleanup? I'm excited just thinking about it. This gives you the time to prepare and complete other tasks from your never-ending checklist. Go ahead and enjoy time spent with family and friends, finish cooking, get your child dressed and ready, or clean the house while a party planner handles the setup, decorating, and breakdown.

Why Hire a Party Planner?

Can you name a business that is more fun and rewarding than the event planning business? Many people have this misconceived notion that event planners are living the dream and life of the rich and famous, and partying with the stars. Nope, it's all an illusion and in your mind. Some companies have noteworthy, celebrity, and well-known clients on their roster but this is not the norm. An event planners primary job is to handle the logistics, ensure you and your guests have a good time, and create a close to flawless experience. You and your guests are partying while we're working hard in the background, ensuring that the timing and flow is seamlessly executed. I've never seen a flawless event, but due to the nature of the business we strive for perfection, and are equipped and ready for the next problem lurking around the corner. We want your guests to have a wonderful experience, and leave happy, talking about your event for years to come. Personally speaking, I strive to over exceed my client's expectations. To accomplish all of this, event planners resemble ninjas, quietly and quickly working behind the scenes to perform our duties. Your guests may not even notice our presence. We keep all the nuts and bolts of the party out of the limelight. If a disaster occurs during setup or during the party, it's our job to think and react quickly to shield the client and guests from the drama. Event planners sometimes get little credit and praise for their hard work, loyalty, and dedication. Being in the limelight is hard work, labor-intensive and stressful, but it's all rewarding at the end when we get praise from our clients and their guests.

An excellent way to make sure your party is a success is by hiring a children's party planner who is equipped and experienced in organizing children's parties. A professional party planner will manage the logistics of the party and handle the decorations, coordinate with vendors, setup and decorate, facilitate and host the party, and cleanup. Some party planners can supply entertainment and catering services, making them a one stop shop when it comes to children's parties. However, most will just refer you to a top-notch vendor on their preferred vendor list. Coordinate with your other vendors and suppliers so all you have to do is sit back, relax, and show up to your own party. Really, it's that simple when you have a party planner on hand. I don't know about you, but being able to breathe and not being stressed is *priceless* in my eyes. I've been on the other side and I've walked in your shoes. The struggle is real.

Are you an all hands on deck type of mom that thinks you don't need a party planner? No matter who you are–novice, intermediate, and professional experts can all benefit from a party planner. Just because you hire a party planner doesn't mean you can't still get involved and get your hands dirty. You are welcome and encouraged to contribute your inputs as to what will likely be best for your child. You know your child better than anybody else, so your feedback will likely be useful and valuable.

Do you want a stress and hassle free party? If so, then hiring a party planner is your key to success. Reconciling a client's vision with a successful end-result is one of the stressful elements of working in event planning. Bringing together ideas and turning them into a functioning, small or large scale event takes a professional.

The great thing about hiring a children's party planner is that they take care of everything from start to finish, or they can pickup where you left off in the planning stage. If you only need day of event coordination, that can be done as well. The most difficult part in organizing a children's party is the execution the day of the event. The day of the party is when everything that could go wrong will, if you have not properly planned. Party planners can do it all. When it comes to entertainment, the possibilities are endless. From executing the party, to facilitating the crafts and games, planners know what it takes for your guests to leave the party entertained and happy. Clients are able to choose from a variety of different themes minus the hassle in executing it.

Parties Are Not FREE

When hiring a party planner you have to manage your expectations. Remember parties are not free. When you hire a party planner you are paying for the experience, knowledge, expertise, and most importantly peace of mind. You are paying for a hassle and stress free party. Event planning is a time consuming, stressful, and labor-intensive work. There are numerous life lessons you can learn about the logistics of planning an event. In most cases, people get their first glimpse of the event planning world when they plan their own wedding. If you have ever planned a wedding you know and understand that planning a party has a ton of moving pieces that all need to seamlessly come together the day of the event.

Remember, once you kick off the party there are no second chances, take backs, or redos, so be sure to make realistic and sensible decisions based off your budget, and not your emotions. Increasing your budget based on emotion is a setup for failure and disappointment.

Stay in Your Lane

Let's say you're planning to host an upcoming party. You've made your party list and checked it twice, however the list continues to get longer because you don't have enough time or energy to complete all the tasks before your party. Those dreaded days of wasting gas and dragging your kids in and out of several stores to find the perfect decorations for your party is a thing of the past. This is where a party planner will come to your rescue.

Anyone can throw a party, but do you really want to do all the running around it takes to make your upcoming party a success? A party planner will eliminate the stress by doing the legwork for you.

Remember, you don't need to have a PhD or be the next "Martha" to have an unforgettable party. Your party planner or event stylist will help you create the overall look and feel by setting the tone of your party, from unique touches that incorporate your personality, to those WOW moments leaving your guests speechless.

Bang for your Buck

Is it possible that a professional event planner can save you money? Yes, it is. Event planners have an abundance of knowledge, experience, and networking colleagues in their back pocket. Party planners have a ton of party décor and props in their inventory and at their finger tips. People spend up to $300 for a specialty cake, $175+ for a character visit, and $125+ for a face painter or balloon twister, so why would you skimp on hiring a professional event planner that will make your life easier and stress free?

Want a specific look? A party planner will know how to find it, where to buy it, how to make it, or where to rent it. Get the high-end look for less by hiring a party planner or event stylist. It can take months or years for a party planner to develop and complete their party themes. Party planners search high and low and go from store to store, and surf the Internet for the perfect party décor on a daily, weekly, or monthly basis. You will most likely not be able to recreate the look and find the exact décor they have in their inventory.

Event Timeline

Here's an example you can use to create your own event timeline.

Time	Agenda	Completed
11:00-2:00 p.m.	Setup and decorating.	☐
2:00 p.m.	Party starts and guests arrive.	☐
2:00-2:15 p.m.	Icebreaker games. (15-minute grace period for late arrivals)	☐
2:15-2:45 p.m.	Facilitated crafts. (20-30 minutes)	☐
2:45-3:15 p.m.	Facilitated games. (30-40 minutes)	☐
3:15-3:40 p.m.	Lunch served. (15-25 minutes)	☐
3:40-4:00 p.m.	Sing happy birthday, blow out candles, picture taking, cake cutting, and serving cake. (15-20 minutes)	☐
4:00 p.m.	Party ends, hand out party favors, and thank guests for coming.	☐
4:15 p.m.	Breakdown, clean up, and relax.	☐

CHAPTER 3
The Perfect Venue

Location, Location, Location

Similar to real estate, location is key when planning a party. You don't want to give your guests any reasons why they don't want to attend your child's party. Be sure the party venue is not over twenty minutes from your home. Fifteen minutes is ideal and thirty minutes is too far for most guests. You can't get mad or expect parents to want to drive thirty minutes to attend a children's birthday party. If I'm driving thirty minutes to a birthday party the venue must be spectacular. If you live in a rural area, it's understandable you will have to travel greater distances. In this case, it's not a deal breaker for your guests.

When choosing a venue, make sure they can accommodate your guests without leaving people feeling cramped, hot or freezing, and irritable. Come on now, we've all been to a party where you wanted to tell the host or venue to open a window or three.

Home Parties versus Venues

For many parents, the convenience, ease, and stress-free aspects of hosting a party at a venue is a winner. Venues offer adrenaline packed activities and fun factor, one stop shop for entertainment, personal party coordinator and party host, and no setup and cleanup. Sounds good right? Venues have to enforce limitations because they host several parties in one day. They have to get you in and out in order to prepare for the next party following yours. Sometimes the warm and fuzzies get missed during the communications because everything is so rush-rush. Parents feel rushed when hosting parties at a venue. When the party is over it's over. You cannot sit around, laugh, and chat with your guests for long before you get kicked out. The staff will break out the vacuum cleaner, dust pan and sweeper, and remove the tablecloths while you're still at the table. Don't be offended, companies mean well, but it's the nature of the business.

If you're hosting a home party, which we love, then you have more control over the logistics of your party. I'm sure you are shaking your head at this moment, and in the back of your mind saying, "You couldn't pay me to have a party at my house." With the right support and help from family, friends, or a party planner, you can host a great home party. There are many advantages to hosting a home party, which includes no guest number restrictions, unsanitary and crowded restrooms, boiling temperatures that will give any woman a hot flash, and parking lot arguments over limited parking spaces.

Unique Venues

A venue is a place where you host an organized event such as a birthday party. Locating a unique and fun venue to host a party can be a daunting and hectic task. It is essential to find a venue that provides most of your party requirements under one umbrella. You can search for different party venues in your vicinity. Be sure to choose the most appropriate package according to your budget and your child's preference. Research the activities and the level of entertainment the venue is going to provide. A well-executed party will complement the mood, fun factor, and aesthetics of your event.

Don't just look at party halls, ballrooms, and traditional venues for rental space. Consider your local community center, museum, zoo, beach, library, public park, restaurant, craft store, etc. Don't forget your backyard and home are always free. Now that's something to cheer about. Who doesn't love free?

Cookie Cutter Venues

Have you ever received a children's birthday party invitation to a popular but oversaturated venue? What was your reaction? Repetition can kill your excitement and joy, especially if it's done over and over again. For some parents and children, being invited to the same venue with the same party theme is boring; they prefer variety. Some birthday party venues are so over populated in the local community, parents just RSVP no.

Choosing the right children's party venue and appropriate theme for the party is key. As kids get bored with the bounce houses and gyms, what venue should you choose? Parents have a difficult time figuring out and choosing the venue for their child's next party. Parents no longer want cookie cutter party venues. They want distinctive and unique party spaces that are fun and memorable. Some great venue options are a trampoline park, paint studio, miniature golf, go-karts, Escape Room, and indoor sky diving. When choosing children's birthday party ideas, keep it simple, unique, and memorable. Choose a theme your child loves, not what you want them to enjoy, or what's trending.

Read the Fine Print

Be sure to read your venue and vendor agreements before signing your John Hancock. Read the fine print and agreements in its entirety, so you don't have any surprises should you have to postpone or cancel your party. If you do not understand the legal jargon, please contact a local attorney. I know this sounds extreme but it's better to be safe than sorry. Some of these legal contracts are so good, you could accidently sign away your first born.

PARTY PLANNING SURVIVAL TIPS

☐ Be prepared for the unexpected. Think fast when problems arise.

☐ Planning parties isn't rocket science so don't overthink.

☐ Outsource tasks to vendors.

☐ Delegate, delegate, delegate. Seek help from friends and family.

CHAPTER 4
You're Invited

Who's Coming?

It's time to create the dreaded guest list. Parents, along with their children, have to decide who to invite, how many people to invite, and who not to invite. There are so many options of who can be invited to a children's birthday party. You can invite girls, boys, or both girls and boys. The total number of friends invited for the party is very important since inviting acquaintances is not always preferred. The more children you invite, the more difficult it becomes to cater to their demands.

Teach your child you cannot invite everyone to their party and, in return, they will not be invited to every party. Children want to belong and don't want to feel alienated from their peers. Children can get very emotional, sad, upset, and will shed some tears when they are not invited to a party. This is the reason why most elementary schools have strict rules where you have to invite the entire class or none. Who really wants to invite twenty-five children your child barely knows or talks to just because they are in their class? You do not have to invite the entire class, but you need to be discrete in how you invite the children. Be selective in choosing your guest list. Invite the ten people who care for your child over the twenty-five people who don't know your child.

The More the Merrier? Wrong.

People use the phrase, "The more the merrier" but do you really want more people? If you invite more people will you be merry? The number of guests invited will determine whether your event will be large and grand, or small and intimate. Can you pull off a small intimate gathering at your home? Sure, but how will you pull off a children's party with sixty guests, sixty chairs, and ten tables? The more guests you invite, the more space, food, beverages, plates, utensils, tables, chairs, centerpieces, and party favors you will need.

Can you afford more guests? You should have a maximum headcount in mind before discussing the guest list with your child. Keeping the guest list to a minimum will save you money. We recommend using the AGE+1 Rule to determine how many guests to invite. This useful rule will keep your guest list in check, so it doesn't get out of hand. Don't be persuaded into hosting more children than you really feel comfortable inviting. If your child insists on inviting a few more children, be ready to negotiate. Sometimes you have to put on your persuasive hat and negotiate with your kids. The more people you invite, the more money you pay for the venue, entertainment, catering, cake, and party favors.

Child's Age + 1

When your children are in pre-school, they don't have true friendships beyond their family members. Children's birthday parties for ages four and under will primarily be family and your friends. As your child gets older and enters elementary school, you may have an increase in your child's circle of friends. When trying to decide how many guests to invite, it's recommended you take your child's age and add one. For instance, if your child is 10, you would invite 11 guests (10 + 1 = 11). When it comes to who not to invite, it can be a touchy and sensitive subject. The good news is that it should be a teaching and learning opportunity for your child. Teach your children early about party discretion. Children should not talk about their party in class or around children not invited. Easy, peasy right. Now you've figured out how many people to invite, the hard part is deciding who not to invite.

The School Dilemma

Many elementary schools have strict rules for birthday parties. Parents must invite the entire class if you want the teacher to pass out the invitations to each student. Yes, you heard me right. You must invite all twenty-five students in your child's class if you want the school involved. Some elementary schools are trying to prevent unnecessary tears and angry moms from popping into the front office when their child did not get invited to a party. As a parent, what can you do? Do you have to invite the class bully just because of a school rule? No, you are not obligated to invite the entire class if you don't want the teacher involved passing out invitations. Stick to your headcount and only invite the children your child wants at their party. The guest list should be created by your child, not you.

Do you know the contact information for each parent? If you have no clue how to contact the parents, you will have to play detective. Try to contact other parents, join the Parent-Teacher Assocation (PTA), look in the PTA student directory, search on social media, or email the room mom.

Custom Invitations

My entrepreneurial journey began in the custom invitation and stationery arena. So I know a little something regarding invitations.

People assume sending invitations is a waste of money and kills trees, but the party starts with the invitation. The invitation is the first thing your guests will see and sets the tone for the party. It shows guests you appreciate and care about them.

Create excitement for your upcoming party by sending custom invitations. You can buy fill in or custom printed invitations. Consider sending Save-the-Date cards for formal events, special occasions, and milestone events. Be sure to mail the invitations two to three weeks before your party. Guests are more likely to attend your party when you create excitement and a buzz around your event. Sending invitations can go a long way with your guests. The invitation may be the one deciding factor whether your guests attend or not attend your upcoming party.

Electronic Invitations

Do you prefer sending electronic invitations? The truth is, as an information technology (IT) professional, I get it. Who can resist the convenience and ease of sending electronic invitations? In today's computer savvy world, more people are opting to use electronic invitation delivery tools to spread the word. People have joined the electronic invitation bandwagon because of the convenience, ease, and cost savings of not having to pay for postage. Another perk is that guests will not misplace or lose an electronic invitation. Sending electronic invitations are budget-friendly or free. Can I get a high five if you love free? Choose your favorite electronic delivery method and get your party started. For celebrating special milestones and formal events, I recommend paper invitations.

The Dreaded RSVP

RSVP stands for a French phrase, "s'il vous plaît". In English it means "Please Respond." As a rule of thumb, guests should respond to an invitation within one week of receipt, or by the RSVP date specified. Unless otherwise stated, you should respond to an invitation whether or not you plan on attending. Who wants to chase down, call, text, and send email reminders to strangers they don't even know. The things we do for our children, right?

Have fun and be playful collecting your RSVP headcount by turning it into a game. On the invitation notate you will give special prizes for the first and tenth guest who RSVP. The number you choose should equal the age your child will be turning.

Accepts with Pleasure

If you RSVP'd yes, your attendance is a commitment and obligation to the host. If unexpected obligations arise, go to the event, give your best wishes, and leave early. The only exceptions and valid excuses are if the guest is sick, called to work, family emergency or obligation, or death in the family. If you RSVP'd yes, you have made a commitment to the host.

Regrets Only

Many guests get confused with the "Regrets Only" call of action. It means you don't have to RSVP if you are attending the party. You should only contact the host if you are unable to attend the party. Otherwise, the host will mark down you will be attending.

Non-Transferable Guests

The invitation is for the recipient only. This means if your name is not on the invitation, you're not invited. You cannot ask someone else to go in your place. Never send someone in your place or invite a guest if you are unable to attend without getting approval from the host. Bringing extra guests puts extra stress and financial burden on the host. You may assume inviting someone to take your place will help the host, but that's not always the case.

Chasing Down Guests

Do you have to chase down a guest to get their RSVP? Failing to RSVP is an epidemic in today's party planning world. We need a call to action and an intervention. As irritating as it sounds, you are most likely going to chase down parents. So here's the deal, most people who fail to RSVP don't intentionally mean to be disrespectful. For most parents, we'll blame it on forgetfulness. Another parent may think it's okay not to respond if they are unable to attend. They assume the party host should know they're not attending if they don't respond. Wrong, you still need to RSVP. Many parents are uncertain if their child can attend due to scheduling conflicts so they wait to RSVP until they finalize their schedule. Some parents don't understand the urgency and importance of RSVPing. Finally, you have parents who just don't care and they do it out of spite. Whatever the excuse, try not to take it personally. Forgetting to RSVP for an event is never a good excuse, but it happens.

Anxiously waiting or tired of waiting for your guests' RSVP? Keep in mind, many guests perceive social media events as being informal and don't take it seriously. Guests may overlook or ignore your invitation and don't RSVP because it's not a priority. Guests that don't value your event are unlikely to RSVP but will show up the day of your party. Try to contact parents by email, text message, social media direct message (DM), and instant message (IM). Most will comply if you send them a reminder. Your guests will appreciate the reminder, and they will be more likely to attend. Email is the preferred method of communication for contacting unfamiliar guests.

Final Headcount

Venues need a final headcount one week or several days before your event. Remind your guests you must give a final headcount to the venue and/or vendors.

If you're hosting a party, only provide the venue with the exact number of guests who RSVP'd. Do not pad the numbers assuming another guest may come. You should not add to or subtract from the guest count after the venue RSVP deadline. Most venues will allow you to increase the guest count because, of course, it's in their best interest to make more money. Use your discretion on how to handle uninvited guests that arrive without RSVPing. You can either tell the uninvited guest you can't have more children because you confirmed the final headcount, or make accommodations with the venue or vendor to add extra guests, which will increase your total cost.

CHAPTER 5
Let Them Eat

Playing Master Chef

Are you a master chef? No, so why are you trying to cook and make gourmet meals the day of your party? I understand doing the cooking yourself saves money but if it stresses you out, take off your chef apron and trash the cooking. Don't take on the responsibility to cook on the day of or the night before your party. Do yourself a favor and outsource the food and buy party trays from your local grocery store or a catering company.

Airplane Food

For formal, extravagant children's birthday parties, the quality of the food you serve is very important for the success of your party. Please don't serve food that tastes like airplane food. I'm sorry but no one wants to eat rubbery, unsatisfying, and inedible food whether it looks fancy or not. Did you know many guests go to parties assuming the food will not taste good? Many of us can admit to eating before or after a party because you're not sure of how the food will taste. I would recommend you attend a food tasting before you hire a caterer or baker. You don't want to be disappointed the day of your event. Your guests will be hungry, unhappy, and you'll have a ton of food leftover because it was terrible.

Fancy Foods

Do you need fancy foods for a children's birthday party? Absolutely not, but kids love creative and personalized foods and snacks you can display at parties. Children are drawn to bright colors and enticed by cartoon-like characters. Make your food kid-friendly and enticing. Play with food coloring. Blue pancakes, why not? It may look gross for adults, but it could be a hit with the children.

Don't spend hours trying to create the perfect homemade bruschetta dish, topped with tomatoes, and drizzled with olive oil. I hope you're making this for the adults because the entire tray will be left uneaten if it's for the kids. Sometimes having sophisticated foods at a children's party doesn't work. If you have fussy eaters, stick to the basics and stay away from spicy or saucy meals.

Many parents think serving elaborate food is over the top and unnecessary. It makes parents feel inadequate and guilty for not hosting upscale parties for their own children. Creating creative and fancy finger foods is not rocket science. At the end of the day, your guests will eat what you serve or starve.

Stain-Free Parties

Many parents have anxiety when hosting parties in their home because of the messes, spills, and stains. In your mind, you have ruined your home before you even had the party. Just face it, you can't have a birthday party without food, beverages, and/or cake. The only way to prevent not having spills and stains is to not have a party. One strategy is to cut any food items that create big messes. Stick to foods which can be handled by children on their own. Don't serve your favorite spaghetti recipe, oily foods, sauces and dressings, and colored punch at your party. Choose dry foods and keep your beverages transparent in color. Who doesn't love chicken fingers, lemonade, and water? Chicken fingers are a winner with children. The kids will return home clean, compared to other messy food options.

Food Allergies

Allergy-free lunch - check. EpiPen - check. Benadryl - check. Vomit bags - check. Inhaler - check. Emergency plan - check. Child in car - check. How many moms can relate? Be warned, many children have severe food allergies and rare diseases which cause allergic reactions. The most common food allergies are milk, eggs, peanuts, fish, shellfish, tree nuts, wheat, and soy. The reactions range from mild to severe which includes sneezing, stomach cramps, rash, hives, swelling, vomiting, and difficulty breathing.

As a mother with a child allergic to almost everything, I put him on medication instead of restricting him from every food known to man. Parents who have kids with allergies, the idea of going to a birthday party can be stressful and exhausting. Many parents feel like they're portrayed as being the overprotective and bossy parent. Are the cupcakes store bought? Is the candy gluten-free? Does the cake contain nuts? Is there any cross-contamination with nuts? May I please see the ingredients? I know these types of questions for an already stressed party host can get frustrating, but the parent means well. Parents are only looking out for the safety and well-being of their child.

Birthday parties are also stressful and disappointing for the kids. Children with allergies don't want to be isolated and singled out from their friends or labeled as the outcast and fun wrecker. What child enjoys not being able to eat the birthday cake? Many children are unable to eat the traditional pizza served at parties. As a guest, communicate with the party host about your child's allergies in advance. Educate your children about their allergies and what they can and cannot eat at the party. Should your child eat before or bring their own lunch? Yes, party hosts are relieved when parents bring their own food and special snacks so it takes the liability and pressure off of them. The last thing a parent wants is for another child to have an allergic reaction at their party.

Pre-Made Cakes

Purchasing a cake from a local grocery store, picking the theme out of a book, with little customizations is not your only option. Nowadays, the craze for children's birthday parties is having tiered specialty themed cakes. Parents are choosing specialty cakes over pre-made grocery store cakes if they're looking for homemade from scratch, tiered layers, unique shapes and sizes, and exotic fillings and flavors.

Fondant Anyone?

Fondant is a popular trend for children's birthday cakes. I have a love-hate relationship with fondant. Fondant makes the most beautiful and amazing cake designs. You've seen them and you know what I'm talking about. Those gorgeous two and three-tiered cakes that look like a wedding cake. Fondant gives your cake a smooth, clean, and polished look. Many parents love fondant icing but children dislike it. There's a reason why it's called sugar paste. Time after time, I have seen children remove the fondant icing from the cake or they comment it tastes like cardboard or sweetened clay. If it's too thick, messy, or difficult to remove, many children won't eat the cake.

Do you love the look of fondant but don't have the budget to buy one? I'm no baker, but there are inexpensive alternatives to using fondant such as buttercream. Which one is the icing on your cake?

People love cake, and they want to taste a delicious, flavorful, and moist slice of cake. Why waste your money and disappoint your guests with a subpar cake? Don't spend $100-$200 or more on a specialty fondant birthday cake if no one will like or eat it. If you must get fondant, ask the baker to create a thin fondant layer so the children will enjoy it. The last thing you want is for the entire cake to be left for you and your family to eat. No thank you, I'm still trying to lose the weight from giving birth ten years ago. If you love the look and taste of fondant, by all means, do what makes you happy. Decide what is more important, the look of the cake, how it tastes, or both. If you're like me, I want the best of both worlds so my vote is for the look and taste.

CHAPTER 6
Are Good Manners Extinct?

RSVP Already

The importance of RSVPing was previously discussed but it's necessary to repeat. One of the biggest complaints I hear from parents is their guests failing to RSVP. For most parents, the RSVP process is one of the most stressful aspects of the party planning process. As a rule of thumb, a guest should respond to an invitation call of action within one week of receipt, or by the RSVP date specified. If you're guilty of being someone who forgets or neglects responding to the RSVP call of action, please stop. When you're invited to an event, you have three choices: 1) Either you don't want to attend, 2) want to attend, or 3) you don't know if you can attend and will respond as soon as you find out. Pick the best option, respond promptly, and get it done. It only takes two to three minutes tops to RSVP, so don't overthink it. Don't be the parent that other parents talk about. Please be courteous and respond to the four-letter RSVP call to action. Don't ignore those four-letter words thinking the host will not care because they do. The party host has every right to gently nudge and send reminders to you until you RSVP. When the shoe is on the other foot, you would respond the same way. You should never contact the host the day before the party inquiring if it's too late to attend. Yes, you've missed the boat and it's too late unless the host says otherwise. Go ahead and ask permission of the host if you want to attend. Worst case scenario, the host will say no. Late RSVPs could cause unnecessary stress for the host and increased expenses because they did not include you in the headcount.

Siblings

Have you ever had an uninvited sibling attend or crash your party? A carefully planned party can fall apart when siblings show up. I'm referring to any toddler or older sibling that will partake in the food and engage in the activities and games. Many parents think the no siblings rule is not polite while party hosts think it's disrespectful for parents to bring uninvited siblings. Who is right?

As a guest, you are not planning and paying for the party. When the invitation lists your child's name only, siblings are not invited. When the words "siblings welcome" are not on the invitation, siblings are not invited. If the party host wanted your five-year-old sibling to attend, their name would be listed on the invitation or electronic invitation. The same goes for your child's best friend, cousin, and neighbor. If their name is not on the list, they're not invited.

Don't take it personally. There are many reasons parents may not want siblings attending (inappropriate age range, per person fees, guest number limitations, space restrictions, limited tables/chairs, food, or favors). Parents should always ask the host in advance if it's okay to bring their child's sibling, relative, or friend. It's not the host's responsibility to figure out babysitting or transportation issues for your other children. If the party doesn't fit into your schedule, then decline the invitation.

For party hosts, when uninvited siblings attend your party, you have two choices. Either allow siblings to join in on the fun, or politely tell the parent the invitation was only extended to the name on the invitation. It's always best to handle the situation to avoid ill-will or negative feelings towards the parents and children. Have a plan for different scenarios so you're not caught off guard and dumbfounded with your mouth wide open. You could choose to flex your hostess muscles and stand firm, but most etiquette experts recommend you step back.

When is it appropriate for a party host to say no to uninvited guests? You are the host, and in return, you may say no. While the rule of thumb is to try to accommodate one uninvited guest, it may get challenging when the host doesn't have enough food, space, party favors, and time to handle and accommodate the unexpected guest. If a guest brings several other people to your party, you are within your rights to say you cannot accommodate extra guests. There will not be enough food for everyone. Multiple unexpected guests showing up at a party is a stressful and unfair burden for the party host.

Your priority is to your guests that RSVP'd. It's important your invited guests are able to eat before uninvited guests. You can decline to serve the uninvited guests if you do not have enough food. If you do not have ample space but want to accommodate the uninvited guest, you can seat the person in another room while the invited guests are at the formal table you planned and prepared for them. The host can also say no to uninvited guests when there might be awkwardness between an invited guest and an uninvited guest. Allowing uninvited guests such as ex-spouses, ex-boyfriends, and ex-girlfriends could create unnecessary drama, tears, and frustration. You don't want to create a tense atmosphere where guests are walking on eggshells because of one uninvited guest.

The success of your party depends on people enjoying each other's company. Unnecessary drama, bickering, and arguing will kill any party before it even starts.

Drop-Off or Not?

Who doesn't love a drop-off party. If you have never had the pleasure of attending a drop-off party, you're in for a treat. Drop-off parties are when the parents will drop off their child at a birthday party and pick them up at the end of the party. Woo-hoo, this means parents don't have to stay at the birthday party. Don't worry, your kids are in a controlled environment and not home alone without adult supervision.

What is the right age for drop-off parties? Parents you are in control of deciding what is the right age for your child. It depends on the child's age, relationship with party host, comfort level, maturity level, and temperament. As a general rule of thumb, children up to age five will attend with their parents. The fun begins around first grade. Most parents drop their kids off between six and seven years old.

Why don't parent's drop-off? For parents with younger children, drop-off parties may be scary and stressful. Many parents assume if they stick around they are helping the host so you don't have to worry about their child if they misbehave or has special needs. Another reason parents stay around at parties is because they have nowhere else to go. It's a waste of gas to go home and come right back to pick up their child. Many parents linger around because they know the parents attending and want to chat. Other parents stick around because they enjoy watching their children having fun, smiling, and laughing with other kids. If you're a parent who stays, it's always courteous to offer to help the host. You're not obligated to join in on the fun and help but it's appreciated.

Most party hosts usually don't want parents staying. Sorry, it's not happening. Parents will not drop-off their younger children with strangers. Although your children may play together, you are a stranger to another parent. We encourage parents to stick around to watch their child for intimidating parties. If you're invited to a pool party and your child is not a strong swimmer, then stay. Parties hosted at well-known venues in a controlled environment, have fewer parents which stay.

The best way to clarify you are hosting a drop-off party is to add the information on the invitation. Add the line, "Parents encouraged to drop-off children. Please drop your child off at 2:00 p.m. and pickup at 4:00 p.m. Parents enjoy your free time." If the venue does not allow parents to stay or they charge per person, you can use the wording, "This is a drop-off party due to the lack of space." For parents too nervous to leave their child at a birthday party, they can opt out and stay in the lobby or in their car. In case of emergencies, leave your contact information with the party host along with any social/behavioral concerns, food or environmental allergies, or medical conditions.

Most parents love drop-off parties. Parents welcome and will thank you for letting them leave. If you're invited to a drop-off party then only drop off the invited child. The host will not appreciate you dropping off your other two children if they were not invited.

No-Shows

Most parents have experienced the frustration of guests not showing up. If parents are planning a party at a children's birthday venue, the host is paying a per child or per person rate. Who likes math? You can't host a party without crunching numbers. If fifteen children confirmed they would be attending your child's party and only ten children show up, the host is still paying for fifteen children. $20 per person which totals $300. Do you want to pay extra money because people don't RSVP? No, who wants to pay more? Once the host submits the final headcount to the venue, they are on the hook to pay for the confirmed number of guests. For some of you, including myself, this is a reminder and flashback of your wedding. The host is out of pocket when people do not show up for the event. If you RSVP'd you will attend a party, but later realize you cannot attend, be sure to contact the host to change your RSVP response. Venues request an estimated headcount two or three weeks before your event, and a final headcount of three to seven days before. Don't wait until the final hour to cancel.

How do you avoid your guests flaking out on you? To reduce the number of no-shows be sure to communicate effectively with your guests and send party reminders one week before the party and on the party day. Many guests will bail on you if a better choice is on the table. Manage your expectations and plan for a 5-20% no-show or last-minute cancellation rate depending on the type of event.

If you find yourself in this situation due to a family emergency, personal health issues, or death in the family, then the host will understand. However, it's impolite and disrespectful to the host to not attend their party because you don't feel like it, you don't feel like buying a gift or you forgot to buy one, you don't have gas in the car, a better event became available, you double booked with another event, you don't feel like driving, its frigid cold or raining outside, you're having a bad hair day, you don't know the other guests, or you have nothing to wear. You may laugh in disbelief, but these are honest confessions why some people will justify not attending a party. If you have to cancel, you need to have a legitimate excuse; death, work, bleeding, or ill. Don't lie or come up with some lame excuse. Tell the truth, apologize, and hope you can make it up to the host. Can you tell no-shows are my pet peeve?

It's natural for the party host to get upset, irritated, and disappointed when people cancel. The host should be gracious in accepting their last-minute cancellation. Give your guest another chance. If they are a repeat and serial last-minute offender, then cut them off for future parties. You can still be friends but without the benefits of getting invited to future events. If you're a last-minute canceler stop. Don't be rude and flake out without having a valid reason. You're wasting the host's money and time.

Party of One

When parents RSVP yes and do not show up at a children's birthday party, it can be a traumatic experience for a child. Your children should not have to deal with the disappointment or heartbreak of no one attending their party. Children want to belong and not feel isolated from their peers. Celebrating a birthday alone is never fun. What if this was your child? How might you react when your child is crying, upset, and disappointed when no one attends their party? Many parents may call it quits and ban future parties to protect their child from being disappointed. It could be your child sitting alone, eating cake alone, and playing games by themselves. Have compassion and think of how it will affect the child before you ditch a party.

Party Crashers

The party is in full swing and one of your invited guests has just arrived with a friend who was not on the guest list, whom you do not know from Adam. While it's considered rude for an invited guest to bring a friend without first asking the host, it does happen. The only course of action now is to kick into full hostess mode and make them feel welcome, or turn them away. How would you handle extra guests and not enough food, drinks, tables, chairs, and party favors? If you're hosting your event at a venue, you will be charged additional fees for extra guests. You should have a plan of how you will handle uninvited guests.

If you play the nice hostess, here are a few tips. For home parties, ask the invited guest to introduce their friend. The unexpected guest may not know anyone at the party. Try to welcome your uninvited guest with a smile without giving them the stink eye or kicking them out. I know keeping your emotions in check may be difficult. You may make a disclaimer to the uninvited guest that he/she is welcome to stay but cannot take part in a craft activity, or take a party favor if you don't have enough. Uninvited guests shouldn't expect to get the same perks as an invited guest. Sometimes guests who RSVP'd they will attend don't show up, so everything ends up working out in your favor. Do what you can to include the uninvited guest in the conversations and games. Finding common ground between invited and uninvited guests are important to making the party comfortable for everyone. Decisions, decisions, but the choice is yours and yours alone.

Dealing with Late Guests

Have you ever had a guest arrive an hour late for your party? How do you handle latecomers? It's unlikely your guests will arrive and hit the doormat at the same time. Many guests choose to arrive late because they do not want to arrive at a party and be the first, second, or third one there. I understand many guests want to be fashionably late, but please don't be over 15 minutes late. Children's birthday parties are only two to three hours long, so if you show up an hour late you missed half the party. Parents are more likely to be on time for parties held at a venue with strict time restrictions and agendas than a home party.

When should you start your party? Always include a party start and end time. The party start time listed on the invitation is the time the party should start. It's understandable to give your guests a 15-minute grace period for arrival. You can't control what your guests do, or don't do, so you might as well plan for the latecomers. You can only control your reaction and response towards the guest, and whether you want to invite them to your next event. I know it's frustrating and irritating, but it's not worth stressing and having a panic attack.

If you're hosting a party, are you always late? Do you advertise the party start time at 1:00 p.m., but don't start the party until 3:00 p.m.? Please don't be late to your own party. You may laugh, but I have seen with my own eyes upset guests leaving a party because the party host and guest of honor were two hours late. Yes, I said two hours late. Please be courteous to your guests and their time. People have other engagements outside of your party, so holding them hostage is not polite.

What if the latecomers are family? We all know and have a family member that is never on time. It can be tricky dealing with family. It's hard to force your family, let alone friends and strangers, to be on time for your party. You have to be honest and truthful about their tardiness. Ask the person if they will arrive an hour early to help you setup. You may get tempted to give your family a different party start time than other guests. Lying about the party start time is not a good option and can backfire.

If you're hosting an event at an expensive venue, you are on the clock and paying for every second you use and don't use. The show must go on, otherwise, you will lose out on valuable time and wasting money. Likewise, if you book a face painter to start at 2:00 p.m., and they start at 3:00 p.m., you will have to come out the pocket and pay for an extra hour. Remember, vendors may have other parties booked after your event, so they must start and end on time according to your agreement. Don't be angry and surprised when you have extra expenses at the end of the event because your party carried over by one or two hours. Don't waste time and money by starting your party late. No matter how hard you try, if you still cannot start a party on time, please hire a professional party planner. Latecomers will have to pick up where you are at the time of their arrival. Never start over or revisit activities for latecomers.

Venues have strict rules with the start and end times. When the party is over, it's over, unless you want to pay for extra party time. The vendors are not responsible when you do not start your party on time. If you need the vendors to stay longer because you did not start on time, be prepared to pay more. Don't negotiate and beg your vendors to reduce the price.

Celebrate the people who came on time, and try not to focus on the latecomers. Try to have compassion when latecomers arrive, no matter what time they arrive. Remember, the person could have ditched your party altogether and not show up, which gets my vote for being inconsiderate and rude without a valid reason. If your guests still arrive late, it's their loss when their child misses out on the fun and is disappointed. Should we have to lower our expectations for our guests' punctuality? No, no, and no.

Sick Kids

Does your child have a nasty cold, fever, chronic cough, or stomach virus? This may be common sense but parents need a reminder. If your child is sick, please have the common decency to leave your sick child at home. Parents bring their snotty nose kids to a birthday party when they're coughing up a lung. Sometimes parents don't know their child is sick because no symptoms exist until the final hour and it's too late. Other parents assume their child is getting over a cold and it's on the tail end. A runny nose and cough may not be a show stopper to one parent but to another, it's a deal breaker. If your child is contagious with multiple symptoms they need to stay home. There is no way to stop a sick child from spreading and passing their germs to the next person. You don't want your child to be the one infecting other children at the party. Happy birthday, my gift to you is the flu.

Early Birds

Are you an early bird for birthday parties? I applaud and respect guests who are punctual and on time. However, parents hosting a party don't have time to entertain and chat if you arrive before the party starts. Parents are too busy with the last minute and final hour setup, food prepping, cleaning the house, fixing their child's hair, getting their child dressed, cooking, or taking family pictures. If the party starts at 2:00 p.m., you should arrive at 2:00 p.m. An acceptable time for early arrival is 5 or 10 minutes early. If you have to arrive early due to conflicting schedules, it's always courteous to tell the host in advance so they can prepare for your arrival. If you arrive too early (15-30 minutes), it's best to wait in the car until the party starts.

Latecomers

Are you a latecomer for birthday parties? The party host has put many hours, time, and money into planning the party. Please do not think you can just show up whenever you want. Children's parties are not open houses where you can come drop in and out as you please. If you're a latecomer, have you ever asked your children how they feel about being late to parties? Their response may shock you when they say it's embarrassing or disappointing because they're always late.

These are teachable moments and life lessons for our children that they too will incorporate into their own lives.

Parents Staying

Do you play rock, paper, scissors, bribe, or negotiate with your spouse to decide who will stay at the birthday party? Moms, do you always get forced to be on birthday party duty? Sometimes parents don't mind staying for ten minutes to play FBI, check out the scene, and to make sure the host is not crazy. Many parents don't want to endure the trauma of having to attend a children's birthday alone. Instead, they tag up with their spouse and attend as a couple to keep each other company. Only one parent should stay for children's birthday parties. It doesn't need to be a family affair.

Small Talk

A birthday party is a great way to mingle and get to know other parents. If you're hosting a birthday party for toddlers or younger children, parent attendance is expected and required. As the host, be prepared to facilitate and entertain the children and parents who stay. Yes, this means you must engage, interact, and create small talk with familiar faces and strangers. If you remember, this was not always the case back in the day. Children's parties were for kids only, and parents just dropped off their children and didn't stay. The world is different today. Those days of leaving your front door unlocked are gone. You can't blame parents for wanting to watch and protect their children.

It can be awkward engaging with unfamiliar faces. Many parents hate the small talk with people they don't plan on talking to after the party. Parents get anxiety being forced to engage in small talk. Starting icebreaker conversations regarding the weather and sports are not fun for parents. Small talk is awkward and unnatural for many parents. These parents prefer to sit in a corner by themselves in silence than being forced to socialize with other parents. Many parents will volunteer to help the party host to keep busy so they don't have to socialize. These parents secretly can't wait for their children to get older so they can drop off their children and run.

Hungry Parents

Greedy parents eating up the party food is a hot topic with many parents. Don't be the parent who is the first one in line to eat at a children's birthday party. We understand you're hungry, but don't take the children's pizza until the host has invited you. At a children's party, unless otherwise stated, the food is for the children, not the adults. If the host orders extra food for the parents, great. However, it's not the host's responsibility to provide lunch or dinner for adults. It's a children's party, so the host doesn't have to feed hungry parents drooling on the sideline. The good news is that most parents offer food for the adults if the children are younger, and they know parents are staying.

Parents, please keep your hunger pains in check. Be courteous and wait for the host to tell parents they may eat. Hold back your cravings and don't run to the food line because you're worried it will run out. This is not an all-you-can-eat buffet, so please be polite and leave food for others. One useful tip for parents is to eat before a children's party in case adult food is not available. Worst case scenario, you can always eat the leftover food from your child's plate.

Pick Up your Kids

When the party is over, it's over. Please don't be the parent always late picking up your child from a birthday party. I understand if it's family, a close friend, or neighbor you know well. If you are a stranger, you need to pick up your child at the end of the party. You don't want your child getting nervous or feeling awkward because they are the last child left and you're thirty minutes late and nowhere in sight. Be sure to let the party host know if someone other than you is picking up your child. If you're running late be sure to call the party host in advance.

PARTY PLANNING SURVIVAL TIPS

☐ Knock out one task at a time.

☐ Turn tasks into family projects and divide the work.

☐ There's no magic trick for planning. Don't reinvent the wheel.

☐ Invest in memories not trends.

CHAPTER 7
The Devil Is In The Details

Don't Believe the Hype

Hooray, you just found the perfect look online. The hard part is recreating the look with your budget. When looking at social media websites for inspiration, be realistic. Recreating the look may not be in your budget. Sometimes these images are oversimplified to make you think any novice can pull it off. Unless you know where to shop, you may not find the same or similar items you see online or for rent. You can try your hand doing a Do It Yourself (DIY) project, but who really has time to spare?

Many clients are overwhelmed, stressed, and overstimulated with the never ending online craft tutorials, event styling, and décor pictures. The décor looks realistic and perfect until you start getting quotes from different vendors on how much it costs to pull off the same look. The lavish event pictures you see online are staged to entice you to take a second look, like or follow the company, and turn you into a paying customer or refer a friend. It's a brilliant marketing strategy. You fall in love with an image, in most cases, you cannot find in the stores or replicate because it's too expensive. In most cases, it's a mystery, and you have to hire a private detective to find and purchase the item online.

You are literally being connected to nowhere. You can get lost in the idea of having the perfect look. The online picture shows the décor for one table. What you forgot to factor into this equation is that you have 120+ guests and 12 tables. I hate to be the bearer of bad news, but I have seen many online inspiration attempts fail. Don't waste your precious time and money searching hours and hours for party décor you cannot find and buy.

Get Unplugged

When you have finalized the party décor, do yourself a favor and unplug from social media. Turn off the notifications and resist the urges to take a sneak peek. Detox, disconnect, and find contentment in your party ideas and stick to them. Seeing your friend's amazing party pictures online will entice you to go bigger, do more, and spend more money. Never look to social media for approval or validation. You don't have to incorporate every décor or craft you've seen on the Internet. Be creative and create your own signature design and fun spin on the party decorations. Don't copy what you see from an image or event designer. Use the image as inspiration and make the design your own.

To DIY or Not to DIY?

Many parents are choosing to try their hand with DIY projects. I get it. Creating crafts and decorations for your child's party is exciting and rewarding. Are you in the running for the 'Mom-of-the-Year' award? Sometimes the DIY act in itself is a thankless deed in the eyes of your children.

Before you decide to DIY, you need to calculate the number of supplies you need for your project, the total cost of the supplies, and the timeframe it will take to complete. Be sure to research and compare the DIY cost, and the expenses if you buy the item at a local store, or online. Unless you love crafting, getting your hands dirty, or you're trying to start a new craft store, most times, you will save time and money buying the party décor in the stores or online. Remember, time is money. If it takes you one to two hours (from start to finish) creating tissue paper pom-poms, it's time spent you can never get back. Sure, it will save you money upfront but it will not save your valuable time which could have been spent with your family. Instead, buy a 6 pack of pom-poms for $5.99. Save your time and energy and buy the party décor items at a local craft store, online, or hire a professional to handle the online shopping for you. If the thought of you having to pull out a glue gun, fabric stapler, and some push pins don't get you excited, then leave DIY projects to the professionals.

Shop with Purpose

Did you know the actual act of researching and gathering information can be a very stressful aspect of party planning? How much gas have you spent going back and forth between the mall, specialty stores, party stores, buying, and returning? Or, how much time did you spend surfing online party stores trying to find the perfect themed decorations? Don't get caught in the trap of impulse purchases online or at your local store. When you first go to the store you should scout out what you need. Take pictures of the décor in the store. Return to the store in one week with a plan and your shopping list. Do not spend your hard earned money on any extras. Stick to your plan and don't deter from your shopping list.

PARTY PLANNING SURVIVAL TIPS

☐ Simple ideas can bring big results.

☐ Don't purchase party supplies that don't add value.

☐ Perfection is not required.

☐ Scale the guest list to fit your space.

CHAPTER 8
The Goody Bag Debate

Where's My Goody Bag?

Some parents call them goody bags and others party favors. You say tomato; I say tamato, but the result is the same. A party favor is a small gift given to guests at a party as a gesture of thanks for their attendance or a memento of the occasion. Parents spend $1-$5 per child towards party favors. Most parties nowadays, a child will not walk away empty-handed.

The high standards and increased expenses for purchasing party favors create unrealistic expectations, added expenses, and pressure on parents. If you have the money to blow, and you want to give a specific high-end favor, do what makes you happy. If you don't have the extra money to spare, don't feel inadequate, obligated, and pressured that you are not giving the kids enough. Why do you feel the kids need more? You've shoved out a ton of money on hosting the party and that in itself is enough. A party favor is not the exchange of a gift for a favor. Don't get it twisted, if you offer a party favor, it does not mean you don't have to send a thank you card to your guest.

We have done a ton of parties and are still shocked when children approach the hosting parents or my team asking for their goody bag before they leave. Societal expectations have children expecting a take home favor bag at the end of a party. Children do not understand the value of money, and sometimes I wonder if they believe it grows on trees. They don't realize the parents hosting the event already shelled out $15-$30 per child to host the party at the venue, and for the pizza and cake they enjoyed. Parents can spend $1,000 or more for a child's birthday party and you still want a goody bag?

Do parents have to provide party favors for guests? No, you are not obligated to send your guests home with a bag of junk. It's a nice gesture to give thanks to your guests for attending but it's optional and not mandatory. When you think about it, the thank you note is where you give thanks and show appreciation to your guests. Party favors are not necessary, but it's always fun for children to receive.

Trash the Goody Bag

I can't say this enough, stay away from the cheap party favors. My frustration with these low-end, cheap toys is that they end up broken before they make it home, or get buried in your children's toy chest never to be found again. Cheap party favors are a waste of money, fall apart when you look at or breathe on it, can be hazardous to babies if swallowed, and have no value. It's a vicious, never-ending cycle. Will you be the one to break the curse?

Party favors were not mainstream back in the day. Parents hosted a party at home or at a children's venue, and the kids played, ate, and then went home. If you don't want to offer a goody bag, say no to the commercial pressure. Many kids enjoy receiving a goody bag and feeling special more than the actual contents of the goody bag. Can we give kids empty favor bags and call it a day? It wouldn't go over well with the kids but it would be hilarious to watch. Goody bags are a rite of passage these days. To break the cycle, you have to stand firm and be willing to say no. You shouldn't feel pressured to offer a goody bag to kids. Never feel guilty, embarrassed, or ashamed for saying no to goody bags. The kids may ask for one but no one will die if they don't get a party favor. You're the host, so the choice is yours. If it makes you feel better, people don't remember favor bags, they remember the experience. That's what a party is all about, right?

Alternative Party Favors

If you decide against spending extra cash on garbage goody bag items, you can still give the kids alternative party favors. My favorite party favor options are personalized edible desserts and snacks such as cookies, cake pops, cupcakes, candy, and popcorn. Gift card favors are trending and are a hit with kids. You can buy small denomination gift cards for $1-$5 per child to your favorite ice cream, froyo, gelato, or Italian ice parlor.

You can also opt for educational and practical favors such as tote bags, canvas hats, activity coloring books, custom crayons, sidewalk chalk,

The Goody Bag Debate

coloring book inspired T-shirts, three-dimensional (3-D) puzzles, inflatable beach balls, jump ropes, hula hoops, stuffed animals, embroidered pencils, pencil cases, bracelets, necklaces, stickers, erasers, bubble wands, flying disc, glitter pens, and sand buckets with shovels.

If you're offering crafts at the party, they can double as take-home favors. Take-home crafts are a hit for children and parents alike. Another tip is to give each child one balloon from your decorations as a take-home favor. You get rid of the balloons and a child leaves with a smile. It's a win-win.

PARTY PLANNING SURVIVAL TIPS

☐ Have your party grocery shopping delivered.

☐ Shop online to reduce stress and save money.

☐ Practice your recipes and DIY projects in advance.

☐ Go to bed early and get plenty of sleep.

CHAPTER 9
Birthday Gifts

Pass the Present-Buying Baton

Buying a present for a child you don't know can be time-consuming and stressful. Parents are tired of running up and down the aisles in order to find the perfect gift. If the gift buying madness is too stressful for you, pass the present-buying baton to your children. Give your child the responsibility and budget to hand pick a present for their friend.

I recommend you find out from your child what the birthday boy/girl likes. If it's too much trouble just wing it. You can't expect parents to know what a child will love from one day to the next. So, what should you buy? Family board games, science experiments, educational toys, activity books, card games, art projects, and kites are always a hit with parents and kids alike. If you can, personalize the gift by matching the party theme.

How Much to Spend

There is much debate on how much to spend for a child's birthday gift. I always say if you give from the heart and stay within your budget then it will dictate what you buy. A thoughtful gift from the heart can be a wonderful treasure to a child. So how much should you spend? I never want to put a price requirement on what a family should pay for a birthday gift because everyone's financial situation is different. The denomination is a personal decision although gifts range from $15-$30.

Children should always be gracious and appreciative when they receive a gift. Teach your children to value the person behind the gift and not the value of the gift. Remember, the real gift is the fun memories that your child and guests made.

No Gifts Please

Your invitation says, "No Gifts Please." What does this mean? What should you do? When a party host says "no gifts", they mean don't bring a gift. There is no reverse psychology or sugar coating with the host's request. Don't over think what it says, it means you don't have to bring a present.

Parents should love this kind gesture but it doesn't feel right to come to a birthday party empty-handed. Is it rude not to bring a gift? Is it rude to bring a gift? Is it rude to not honor the host's wishes? Should you bring a small token of appreciation? Don't worry, you are not rude if you don't bring a gift because you are following the party host's instructions. Despite what the invitation says, many parents will opt to bring a gift for the family and not geared towards the child. If you're determined to bring a gift or token of appreciation, opt to bring a heartfelt birthday card with a pack of stickers, family friendly gift card, beverages, or appetizer. You can also donate a toy to a local charity in the birthday child's name. Don't forget you can offer your services to help at the party.

Charitable Gifts

Does your child own every toy or gadget imaginable? Are you financially blessed? Does your child need more gifts? Ditch the guilt of your child having too many gifts, and bring happiness and joy to others, by donating your toys to charity. Sometimes we need to sit back and remember it's not all about us. It's always better to give than receive.

A thoughtful spin on gift giving is to tell guests not to bring a gift for the birthday boy/girl, but instead, donate a gas card or grocery store card to a local charity of your child's choice. Many charities have opportunities for your guests to donate online. Some charities to check out are the Children's Hospital, animal shelters, zoos, parks, homeless shelters, etc. Parents will thank you for giving them an opportunity to support a local charity. This option lets parents off the hook for having to spend their time shopping from store to store to find the perfect gift for your child. Sign me up.

Gift Registry Debate

Remember the days when children's birthday parties were a simple occasion but packed with fun? Birthday parties are becoming so over the top parents are creating gift registries. Yes, you heard me correctly. The topic is debatable so I will give you both sides.

I understand the logic behind creating a registry. Registries can be a helpful resource for immediate family, grandparents, aunts, and uncles inquiring what your child wants. We don't expect to see a Gucci handbag or spa gift certificate on the registry. Proponents of children gift registries claim it's helpful for parents wanting to buy a parent-approved gift. Many parents hate grabbing a toy off the shelf with little or no thought or meaning.

Most parents think the gift registry trend is presumptuous and rude. Sending out a link to your child's gift registry to guests is a No, No. Never include a gift registry on the invitation. It implies you expect a gift, which is not proper etiquette, whether or not you follow etiquette.

Are you on board with birthday gift registries or do you find it obnoxious? No thank you, I'll pass on this trend. Call me old school, but people need to be gracious for all things given to you. I teach my kids; you get what you get. You receive gifts with a smile whether you like or hate it. Am I right or old fashioned in my thinking?

Gift Card Debate

Do you love or hate giving gift cards for a child's birthday gift? Many parents feel it's impersonal and tacky and others prefer and love them. We found younger kids prefer receiving gifts because it's instant gratification and something they can see, touch, and play with. The older children are, the pickier they get. Older kids prefer cash or gift cards so they can pick out their own gifts. Tweens and teens prefer to buy what they want than to get a gift they will not use, or will return to the store.

Do you worry the gift card goes into the parent's pocket and the kids get nothing? It's a valid point, but it's above my pay grade to stress about something out of my control. Once I give the gift to the person it's out of my hands (literally). In good faith, you have to trust parents will do the right thing for their child.

I have no gripes or problems with gift cards. Gift cards are accessible at most local stores. Just because you buy a gift card doesn't mean it's a thoughtless gift. If the birthday boy/girl likes video games, buy a gift card to a video game or big box retail store that sells video games. You can't go wrong buying a gift card to a local or online bookstore, Froyo or ice cream parlor, movie theater, miniature golf, trampoline park, and waterpark. Nowadays, what kid wouldn't love a gift card from their favorite store so they can get what they want? Gift cards are as good as getting cash. Money is money whether it's in the form of plastic or paper. Good luck on your gift card hunt.

Gift Opening Debate

Do you let your child open presents at the party? This is another hot and debatable topic for parents. Many parents think opening gifts in front of your guests is a tradition. Yes, the kids love seeing the expression and look on the birthday boy/girl's face when they open the gift they bought. Parents feel it is proper etiquette, respectful, and good manners to open the birthday gifts while the guests are present. Children enjoy opening gifts during the party. They get excited by seeing the reaction and expressions on the child's face. When this is taken away, they may feel disappointed because they took the time to pick out the perfect gift for your child.

If you're on board with opening gifts during the party, create a sense of order by having the children sit in a circle. The children can pass around a gift and when the music stops, the child holding it opens the gift and gives it to the birthday boy/girl. You can also put a fun spin on gift opening by passing out the party favors during this time so the kids have something tangible in their hands.

Playing devil's advocate, many parents are skipping opening gifts during the party. There are many reasons parents have turned away from this old tradition. For one, parents think it's time-consuming when the party is at a children's venue. Another reason is that children have a sense of ownership when they see toys, which gets frustrating for parents and the children. Many parents want to use that time to entertain and cater to their guests. Opening gifts can create embarrassment when the gift is unwanted, redundant, or a parent did not bring a gift which may make them feel singled out. Plus, it can create competition and jealousy with other kids.

Have you ever been to a children's party and one kid tries to open your child's gift, or they break the gift by accident? Many kids can't control the impulse to open someone else's toys and tears may shed when they can't play with the toy. It can be tricky depending on the age range of the child. Younger children cannot hide their emotions, boredom, and disappointment. They speak their mind and tell you how they feel no matter if it hurts or not.

Are you in a rush for time? If so, skip opening the gifts until after the end of the party and guests have gone home. Opening gifts after the party can be a great after party treat for the birthday boy/girl. Go with what works best for your family and child.

Are we doing a disservice to our children and giving them fewer opportunities to be gracious? Are we treating the gift opening tradition as a stressful activity when it's not that serious? Whether you embrace the tradition of opening gifts with your guests or make it a private activity after the guests leave, the choice is yours. Whatever you decide, it's helpful to go over birthday party etiquette and good manners with your children before the party.

PARTY PLANNING SURVIVAL TIPS

☐ Presentation matters. Keep it simple, creative, and unique.

☐ Let go and bring out the inner child in you.

☐ Open the door with a smile.

☐ Relax and have fun.

CHAPTER 10
It's Party Time–Let's Do This

Bulletproof Parties (Keep Dreaming)

If you think parties are bulletproof, then keep dreaming. Unexpected challenges are a part of event planning. The key to your success is how you react, respond, and handle and mediate the problem. Early in the planning stages, consider what may go wrong and how you can resolve the problem. Prepare and plan for the unexpected and have a backup contingency plan. If you keep a calm and cool demeanor, your guests will never notice.

Delegate, Delegate, Delegate

Between demanding careers and extracurricular kid activities, when do you really have time to plan a party? The power of delegation is a very useful skill if you want to throw a successful birthday party for children. Exercise your voice by asking family and friends to arrive early and/or stay later to help the children with crafts and games, serving food to guests, and cake cutting. This allows you to focus on everything running smoothly.

The Early Bird Gets the Worm

Feeling tired, exhausted, and overwhelmed the day of the party? Do you stay up late to cook, clean, and complete last-minute tasks? Early in my party planning career, I stayed awake until the wee hours of the night (2:00–3:00 a.m.) to prep for my client's parties. My body was drained and exhausted. When your body talks to you please listen. I knew in my mind if I continued on this track my body would give out and my business would suffer. Determined to change my routine, I set a specific time to go to bed and wake up one to two hours earlier. I discovered I was more energized, alert, and less stressed when I went to bed earlier. Make it a habit to go to bed early and wake up one to two hours earlier. You will feel refreshed and will get much more done. Try it out. Worst case scenario you will get more sleep and feel better.

Plan B (Backup Contingency Plan)

When all else fails, go with Plan B. Not only do you need a Plan B, you should also have a Plan C, D, and E for no-shows, guests that didn't RSVP who attend, uninvited guests, and last-minute cancellations. A backup plan is also needed for vendor cancellations, equipment failures, climate control, medical injuries and emergencies, food and beverage shortages, and natural disasters. Be prepared and ready to move your event indoors or to a secondary location due to inclement weather. Communication is imperative for a successful event. Be sure to have all your vendor phone numbers stored in your cell phone.

CHAPTER 11
The After Party

The Dreaded Cleanup

Congratulations, you survived the party madness. The aftermath and dreaded clean-up duty is a necessary evil. The process of cleaning up can cause exhaustion and stress. At some point after the party, when you're finding empty cans and paper plates stashed in your bookshelf, you have to think to yourself - was all my running around worth the time and stress of this after party cleanup duty? The answer is yes. It's all worth it. All the running around, stress, planning, and clean-up is worth it if it made your child smile and laugh. The key is to find ways and strategies to reduce the stress on yourself.

Need Help? So, Ask for Help.

After the last person leaves your home or venue, it's cleanup time. This is the very moment when you wish you had hired a party planner or cleaning company. Make sure you solicit family and close friends to help with moving and re-arranging the furniture, mopping, vacuuming, washing dishes, and cleaning. Better yet, get those children to work. Teach the kids to be part of the cleaning team. Make cleaning up fun and not a dreaded chore. Play cleaning games, relay music challenges, and contests to earn medals and prizes to ensure their success. As a special treat, have a dance party when you've finished cleaning.

If you would like parents to help you with the cleanup, be sure to ask before trying to crack the whip. Many parents love to help but don't ask because they don't want to get in the way. If parents refuse to help, please keep in mind they have that right and they are considered guests first. So please don't penalize a parent for not offering their assistance to help you even if they made the mess. It's not their party or responsibility to help you clean. If a parent offers their help, by all means, take them up on this offer. You never, and I mean never, want to turn down a helping hand. Never refuse getting the help when its offered even if you feel you can do it yourself. The words, "I don't need any help, I'll get it later." should not be coming out of your mouth. If they were kind enough to offer, you're kind enough to accept.

One helpful tip is to never use your fine china and everyday dishes for a children's party unless the party theme requires real china (e.g. tea party). Make sure you use utensils, plates, or cups which can be disposed of and tossed out. Stay away from the fancy stuff and stick to paper plates. There's no need to run up the water bill cleaning dishes. Using disposable paper products, your guests have no excuse to not clean up after themselves.

I know you're Supermom, but there's no need to be up at midnight cleaning up after others. Plus, no one wants to get up the next day to clean. If you're still cleaning on day three, ask for help. Many moms trap themselves in a corner by having the Supermom mentality of "I can do everything myself and conquer the world" attitude. The best party hostesses learn the value and power of delegating work. Don't feel too proud to take off your cape now and then and ask parents to help. Calling all Supermoms to help could be the saving grace you need from having a total meltdown or losing your sanity.

Cleanup after Yourself

Cleaning up after any party should not be a hassle or last longer than two hours. Provide guests with the ease of cleaning up after themselves by using paper plates and having a trash can accessible. After all, you're the one who's done all the real hard work up to this point. Why should you be left holding the trash bag?

Hire a Cleaning Service

Feeling overwhelmed and too exhausted to clean after a party? If you don't want to lift a finger, consider hiring a cleaning service in advance to come the same day, or next day after the party. If hiring a cleaning service will prevent you from being stressed, it's well worth the investment.

To Send or Not to Send

Woo-hoo, you have planned and executed a fabulous party. Now, what is left to do? Don't forget to give thanks for the gifts your child received. It's very important to take the time to thank your guests for celebrating with you and their generosity. Remember, your guests put a lot of thought into buying a gift. They go from store to store trying to find the perfect gift your child will love.

Giving thanks after receiving a gift is not an old school or outdated tradition. It is always in style to give thanks to someone. You should always thank the person who gave you a gift. Many guests would be hurt, offended, and turned off if you don't thank them. It's not uncommon for parents to even carry a grudge should you forget to thank them. Many people will even stop giving gifts to an unthankful party host. Yes, it's that serious depending on the person. For the older generation or people who follow proper etiquette, it's recommended and expected that you send a handwritten note or thank them by telephone or in person.

Don't feel like sending traditional thank you notes? Do you think it's a dreaded obligation? Try not to think of it as a chore, but a way to show gratitude and appreciation. Purchasing thank you notes will set you back $5-$10 a pack. Write your thank you notes two to three days after the party. You may get too busy with the next hot thing on your never-ending to-do list. Don't put it off because you will forget. A good rule of thumb is for your guests to receive their thank you notes within two weeks. If thirty days have already gone by, go ahead and send the thank you cards. It's better to be late than never. Any type of thank you note is better than nothing at all. Here's a rundown and some quick tips on how to handle the thank you notes.

In Person – If you open the gift in front of the giver, then a verbal thank you will suffice. It's always nice to send a handwritten note thanking the person after the party.

Handwritten Notes – Do you have to send formal thank you notes? I know a handwritten note with today's technology may appear old school, but it's still proper etiquette, personal, and appreciated. Think of it this way. If a person can take the time to go from store to store to find the perfect gift, buy the gift, and wrap the gift, you can at least send a thank you card. Just my two cents but you have to decide for yourself.

By Phone – If you know your guests well, you can thank them by phone. Did I mention calling is FREE? You don't want to call parents if you barely know the person. This option only works well if you have a relationship with the guests and know their telephone number.

If you do not have the physical address of your guest, and only have an email address, your only option is to email a thank you note or send the guest an email asking for their home address. Most people will opt for emailing the thank you note. You can make the email more personal by attaching pictures from the party, or specific pictures of their child.

Ecards – You can send a thank you card in minutes with ecards. Similar to email thank you notes, ecards are informal and generic. Personalize your card by adding pictures, videos, or special messages.

Text Messages – Sending a thank you note by text message is considered a casual form of giving thanks. Many etiquette experts suggest it's not an ideal way to give thanks. Some guests would roll their eyes and perceive sending a text thank you note as being effortless, impersonal, lazy, and cheap. Proceed with caution. When in doubt, pick up the phone and say thank you or stick to the old-fashioned pen and paper method.

CHAPTER 12
The Good, Bad, and Ugly

Love It or Hate It

Congratulations, you made it this far (standing ovation). You have officially survived the craziness of planning, facilitating, and executing your event. It has been an incredible journey writing this book. I hope you enjoyed some of the common reasons parents hate to plan birthday parties. Think about it. Children wait an entire year to celebrate their birthday. Whether it's low key or over the top, kids will always enjoy birthday parties. A birthday party in the eyes of a child is like having the ultimate playdate with all of their friends present instead of just one. Not to mention, you get to play games, eat pizza and cake, and receive gifts. You had me at eating cake.

Despite the good, bad, and ugly of party planning, it's here to stay. When you become a grandparent, you will still celebrate the same birthday parties which frustrated and irritated you with your own children. Our children grow up fast and they will not always be around to spoil.

Children's birthday parties don't have to be an annual occasion. Tell your child they can only celebrate their birthday bi-annually, every five years, or for a milestone birthday. You can also host an intimate birthday party and allow your child to celebrate with a few of their best friends. Worst case scenario, bribe your kids to choose between a family trip or a party. Come on, we've all bribed our kids at one point.

To be honest, it doesn't take much to make a child laugh and smile. When children are surrounded by their family and friends, they're content and happy. Remember, the party will be over in the blink of an eye. Children won't care if all the plates aren't color coordinated, or the tablecloth is too short. They are there to have fun, eat lots of yummy food, and play with their friends. Facilitating the games, crafts, entertainment, food, decorations, and music is often too stressful for most parents. Ask for assistance from a professional children's party planner. With the help of a expert, you can execute the theme you have in mind, along with the perfect age-appropriate games and activities for your guests.

Do you love it or hate it? Are you going to hang up your party planning hat or stay in the game? Maybe you've decided to pass the party planning baton to your spouse or child. I hope there is a little glimmer of hope for some of you. The only way to avoid birthday parties is to avoid them altogether. You can run and hide, but parents can't avoid birthday parties forever. For your own sanity, try to embrace the children's birthday party craze and keep your emotions in check. Our children are only little for a short period of time, so why not make them feel special. Can we all agree we love our kids and want to see and make them happy? Sometimes we have to sacrifice our own happiness for our children. The choice is yours. You can do it yourself or hire someone to do it for you. You know where I cast my vote. After reading the book, I know you already know what to do…hire a party planner. I'm going to say it again. Hire a party planner. So, go ahead, have fun, and enjoy the ride. Cheers to planning a fabulous party.

THANK YOU

Dear Party People,

Thank you for taking the time to read my book and getting to know a little more about the good, bad, and ugly of the children's party planning world.

I hope you enjoyed reading my book as much as I loved writing it. So how did you enjoy the book? I welcome your feedback and would like to kindly ask you to leave a review for *'Why Parents Secretly Hate Children's Birthday Parties'*.

Don't keep this book a secret. Everyone knows someone that could benefit from this book. There is no reason for people to struggle alone or in silence. Thank you for spreading the word and sharing.

Join the party club and sign up at www.partysticklers.com/sign-up/ to stay connected and for a chance to win a free signed copy, giveaways, and printable party planning checklists.

Thank you again for your support. I would love to hear your stories. Keep in touch.

Happy planning,

Ashia Watson

www.partysticklers.com

PRAISE FOR WHY PARENTS SECRETLY HATE CHILDREN'S BIRTHDAY PARTIES

"I love this book! It's well-written, fun, entertaining, and hilarious. What more could you want?"

- Dennis Stanley, Owner of Chantel's Bakery

"Reading Chapter 1 gave me a chuckle! As a cake decorator, I can immediately tell the personality trait of the party mom based on the design of their cake."

- Camille Wider, Owner of Sweet Cakes

"I am thankful for the wisdom and expertise that Ashia shares in her timely book on party planning. It gives parents the confidence and skills needed to plan and implement a successful event that will be remembered for years to come."

- Paula Wilcox, Owner of Imagine Entertainers

"Party Sticklers has always come through for my dance studio. Our events are sometimes planned last minute and Ashia turns my vision into reality in a matter of days with little direction. The owner is very flexible, understanding, creative, and passionate."

- Chequena Morris-Hall, Owner of Elite Formation Studio of Dance

"Ashia's attention to detail, creativity, and professionalism makes the planning process a breeze. She takes the stress of planning, organizing, and orchestrating birthday parties off of the host."

- Elaine Jenkins, Owner of Dabbledy Doo Face and Body Art

"What a great way to turn 50, release a new book and not have to worry about what color napkins I needed. Party Sticklers was great to work with. Their take control and relax and focus on you at the event was welcomed. After our first meeting, I knew I was in capable hands."

- Mark Wiggins, Author

"Ashia the owner of Party Sticklers was amazing when it came to coordinating my daughter's 3rd birthday party! At the end of the party there were a few kids that cried because they had such a great time and didn't want to leave, with that being said Party Sticklers definitely came and delivered a great party."

- Shiloh Family

"I contacted Party Sticklers via email to inquire about planning my daughter's 9th birthday party. When the kids arrived they were all yelling "Awesome!" "Wow!" The party planner was a wonderful host. The girls adored her. I couldn't have asked for a better experience for my daughter (or me!). I'll be contacting Party Sticklers for my future parties, without question. How did I ever have a party without them?"

- Nader Family

"A party by Party Sticklers is the best one a family could ever have. Ashia exceeded all my expectations. The moment I walked into the clubhouse for the party, I was in awe. She transformed the venue into a dreamy space I never would have imagined. Words are not enough to describe the product that Ashia came up with. She has gone the extra mile to do every little item and detail we agreed on. She gave us more than what she was contractually obligated to do so. I think she will outdo herself with every new party she does in the future."

- Lazaro Family

"Party Sticklers is a true gem to the DMV area. I will be consulting with Party Sticklers for my next baby shower, as I am expecting again, and I will be using them for my children's birthdays in the future. I can't imagine planning a party without them. This company sets the standard for parties and events and really takes your event to a whole other level. Thank you Party Sticklers for making my first baby shower a true success!"

- Pettway Family

"I consulted with Party Sticklers for my daughter's 2nd birthday. The party planner contacted me quickly and I shared my ideas for the party which was a month away. We discussed several days prior to the party

Praise

that it might be a possibility that I would need to cancel due to the weather. I decided to not postpone and she came to my house ready to decorate. Traveling more than an hour away, she came through even as several inches of snow was falling on the ground!! I was impressed with the decor and crafts that she had planned. My daughter was so elated and that was ALL that matters."

- Canjura Family

"She made my vision come true. All the children had such a blast. One of my friend's said that this was the best children's party she has ever attended. So it says a lot about Party Sticklers' commitment to making the party perfect."

- Bhattacharya Family

"Ashia did a fantastic job putting together my daughters first birthday party. August tends to be the busiest time of the year for me at work, as much as I love throwing parties. I really just did not have the time to get it together. Party Sticklers was exactly what I needed."

- Atnafe Family

"I cannot say enough great things about Party Sticklers! Not only is Ashia a joy to work with, but she's totally on her game - always bringing great ideas to the table and a level of detail and organization that is above reproach."

- Talley Family

"I recently attended a party planned and hosted by Party Sticklers, and all I could say was WOW! The Monsters Bash theme was incorporated into every detail from the spectacular decor, crafts, games, to even the contingency plan when the rain started midway through the party! The party hostesses didn't miss a beat. They kept the children active, engaged, and happy throughout the full 2 and a half hours, which is no easy task for a group of 5 to 8-year-olds! Perfect execution from start to finish - Party Sticklers is a class act. I will definitely hire them for my next party!"

- King Family

ACKNOWLEDGMENTS

Thank you, God for blessing me with creativity and vision. I never imagined falling in love with event planning, but with God all things are possible.

I would like to acknowledge my wonderfully supportive husband and best friend. You are doing a fabulous job caring and raising our two boys. Together, we make a great team. Thank you for being a role model and leading our family by example with your encouragement, love, and support. I'm blessed that you are my husband and our children are fortunate that you are their father.

Thank goodness for boys. I thank God for choosing me to be your mother. It is my honor and privilege to call you my sons. I love you. There is never a dull moment with you in my life—you keep mommy smiling and laughing. Thank you for helping me with my parties even though I have to pay you.

A special thank you to my parents for your unwavering love and support. Without your words of wisdom and guidance, I wouldn't be who I am today. Thank you for being wonderful parents and amazing grandparents to my children. I appreciate all you have done and continue to do for us.

I would like to thank my Editor-in-Chief, Cathy Oasheim. I appreciate your expertise, guidance, contributions, constructive criticism, and countless nights spent answering my endless emails. The editing process was daunting but we made it. I'm grateful to have you on my team.

A warm and gracious thank you goes out to Althea Watson, Charles Ellerbe, Rickey Macklin, and Michaela Link Brown for critiquing the book.

I especially want to thank my family, friends, mentors, business partners, and clients for motivating me to press forward during this crazy journey called entrepreneurship. I appreciate your kind words of wisdom, advice, constructive feedback, and referrals.

ABOUT THE AUTHOR

Ashia's crazy passion for parties, entrepreneurial spirit, expressing her creativity, bringing people together, and making people smile and laugh, led her to create Party Sticklers. By day, she works a 9-to-5 as a software engineer, with a Master of Science degree in Communications Technology. Ashia knows what it takes to manage a work-life balance, family, and business. She transforms into the Party Girl on the weekend.

Ashia is a party enthusiast and loves the rush and thrill you get when planning parties. She's running towards the craziness and fire when everyone else is running away or screaming for help. After all the craziness is said and done, she wants to do it all over again. Now, that's passion.

Ashia loves spending time with her supportive husband and is the proud soccer mom of two energetic boys that keep her on her toes and in touch with her inner child.

The author is available for public speaking engagements for crafting workshops, parenting and mom groups, motivational, keynote, talk radio, and public appearances.

Visit Party Sticklers at www.partysticklers.com. Follow and like us on Facebook, Instagram, YouTube, Twitter, LinkedIn, and Pinterest @partysticklers.

www.ingramcontent.com/pod-product-compliance
Lightning Source LLC
Chambersburg PA
CBHW050443010526
44118CB00013B/1656